TRENT 1475

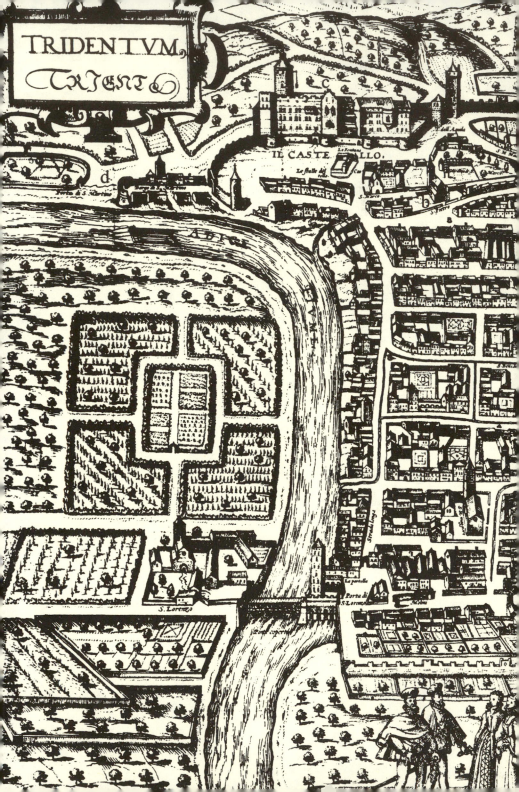

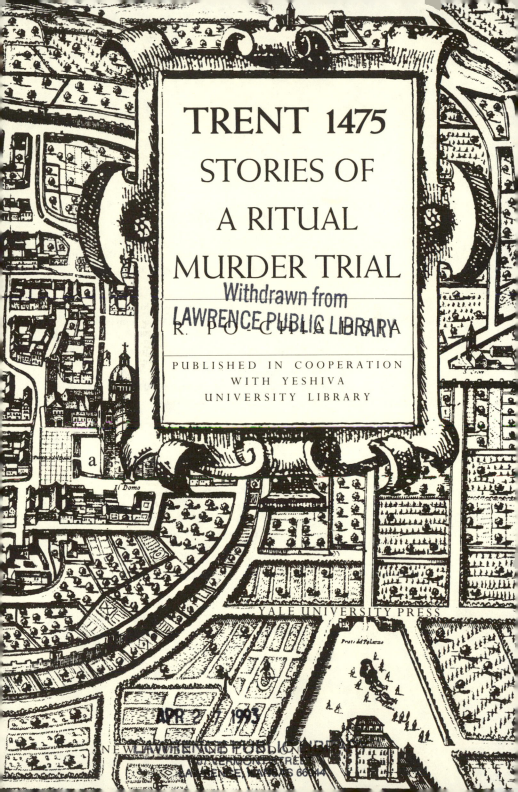

TRENT 1475

STORIES OF

A RITUAL

MURDER TRIAL

R. PO-CHIA HSIA

PUBLISHED IN COOPERATION
WITH YESHIVA
UNIVERSITY LIBRARY

a

Il Domo

YALE UNIVERSITY PRESS

Prato del Palazzo

Published with assistance from the Jesselson Foundation.

Engraving of Trent by Franz Hogenberg, 1588. Noted on the engraving are: (a) the cathedral; (b) St. Peter's church; (c) the Castello Buonconsiglio; (d) St. Martin's Gate. Reproduced courtesy of Provincia Autonoma di Trento, Museo provinciale d'arte.

Designed by Nancy Ovedovitz and set in Perpetua type by The Composing Room of Michigan, Inc., Grand Rapids, Michigan. Printed in the United States of America by Book Crafters, Inc., Chelsea, Michigan.

Library of Congress Cataloging-in-Publication Data

Hsia, R. Po-chia, 1955–
Trent 1475 : stories of a ritual murder trial / R. Po-chia Hsia.
p.   cm
Includes index.
ISBN 0-300-05106-9
1. Blood accusation.   2. Jews—Italy—Trento—Persecutions.   3. Simon, of Trent, d. 1475.   4. Trento (Italy)—Ethnic relations.
BM585.2.H75   1992
945'.385—dc20   92-4612
                                                                         CIP

A catalogue record for this book is available from the British Library.
The paper in this book meets the guidelines for permanence and durability of the Committee on Production Guidelines for Book Longevity of the Council on Library Resources.

10   9   8   7   6   5   4   3   2   1

IN MEMORY OF MY FATHER,
WILLIAM TSE-MING HSIA,
1928 — 1990

CONTENTS

CONTENTS

CONTENTS

ix

ILLUSTRATIONS

FOREWORD

More than five hundred years ago, the Jewish community of Trent was victimized by the accusation of ritual murder. "Prozess gegen die Juden von Trient," an elaborate manuscript account of those tragic circumstances, forms the basis for the present volume, which examines the events and describes the participants, both accusers and accused.

Yeshiva University received this manuscript in 1988 as a gift from Erica and Ludwig Jesselson, universally acknowledged patrons of Jewish culture—its artifacts, its spirit, and its future. The manuscript was presented with the hope that the stories it records would be heard. Good fortune led us to Ronnie Po-chia Hsia, whose response to the challenge was executed with enthusiasm and the dignity of true scholarship.

Our gratitude to all.

Pearl Berger
*Benjamin Gottesman Librarian
and Dean of Libraries, Yeshiva University*

ACKNOWLEDGMENTS

I am grateful to Pearl Berger, Benjamin Gottesman Librarian at Yeshiva University, for inviting me to study the manuscript newly acquired by the university, and to her and David Berger of Brooklyn College for their gracious hospitality during my research visit in New York. The project was helped along the way by Anna Esposito of Rome and Diego Quaglioni of Trent, who are in the process of publishing a three-volume edition of the Latin manuscript records of the trial and other related documents. To Professor Quaglioni and Professor Iginio Rogger of Trent, I owe the honor of an invitation to attend the international conference on the life and work of Johannes Hinderbach held in October 1989. Many people contributed to the work with ideas, suggestions, questions, favors, and information, including Alan Dundes, Stephen Greenblatt, John Harris, Alfred Haverkamp, Penelope Johnson, Bruce Kupelnick, Kate and Michael Langen, Alison and Gordon Weiner, Charles T.

Wood; students in my graduate seminar on early modern Europe at New York University, in particular David Lederer and James Palmitessa; lecture audiences at Dartmouth College, New York University, the University of California at Berkeley, and the University of Trier; and the anonymous reader for Yale University Press.

For institutional support, I am indebted to Yeshiva University Library, Yeshiva University Museum (especially to its director, Sylvia Herskowitz), the helpful staff at the Archivio di Stato in Trent, the Österreichische Nationalbibliothek, and to the Interlibrary Loan department staff at the library at Dartmouth College. The University of Massachusetts at Amherst and the National Endowment for the Humanities provided generous travel support.

Pamela Crossley has been a constant companion during the trying times when this manuscript was being written. These words are meant as a token of my gratitude and affection.

Norwich, Vermont
Spring, 1992

INTRODUCTION

A German manuscript of the ritual murder trial of Trent that was acquired in December 1987 at an auction at Sotheby's was presented in 1988 to the library of Yeshiva University in New York.[1] Copied by one person, in standard late fifteenth-century German chancery hand, the Yeshiva manuscript (YM) consists of 614 folios, numbered consecutively by the copyist. Illuminated initials are found throughout the manuscript. In addition, folio 2v contains illuminated borders in gold, red, blue, and green and also the coat of arms of the house of Württemberg. At the top of this folio, written in a different hand, is a marginal inscription that shows the later provenance of the manuscript: "Conventus vindobonensis carmelitorum Discalceatorum." The leather binding bears the year 1615, which is the probable date when the Viennese convent acquired the text. The manuscript text, written in black ink, is interspersed with notations in red ink.

The YM was copied sometime after 20 June 1478, the date of the papal bull that exonerated Bishop Johannes Hinderbach of any impropriety in his conduct of the trial against the Jews of Trent. It most likely was commissioned during the second half of 1478, or, at the latest, during 1479. There is no firm evidence regarding the genesis of the YM, but either of two people plausibly could have commissioned the manuscript. One was, of course, the count of Württemberg, Eberhard the Bearded, founder of the University of Tübingen, whose coat of arms is depicted in the manuscript; the other was his brother-in-law, Cardinal Francesco Gonzaga, bishop of Mantua and canon of the cathedral of Trent. Thanks to Mantegna's frescoes, we have vivid portraits of the Gonzaga family: the father, Duke Luigi III; his consort, Barbara of Brandenburg; and their children, including the third son, Francesco, and a daughter, Barbara, who married the bearded count. To celebrate his marriage, Eberhard traveled to Italy, arriving in Mantua in April 1474. If he took the Brenner Pass across the Alps, the traditional route of the German kings, he must have passed through Trent. Thus, when the ritual murder trial commenced in March 1475, Eberhard would have remembered the city on the Adige River. In any event, it is reasonable to assume that the initial repository of the YM was Eberhard's personal library in Stuttgart.[2] Undoubtedly, the ritual murder trial in Trent turned the count decidedly against the Jews within his own domain: when Eberhard founded a university in Tübingen in 1477, he also expelled all Jews from the town; and in his testament of 1492, Eberhard forbade Jews to reside or trade in Württemberg.[3]

We cannot document how the manuscript was transmitted from Stuttgart to Vienna. Presumably, the Carmelite convent acquired the manuscript as a gift. But from whom? One might speculate that the imperial family was the patron. The Habsburgs could have acquired the manuscript during their occupation of Württemberg (1520–1534), after Duke Ulrich was deprived of his title by an imperial ban, for murdering one of his knights. The manuscript might have been transported to Vienna after the capture of Stuttgart in 1534 by Imperial troops. At any rate, we know that from 1615 to 1930, the YM remained in the Carmelite convent in Vienna. At the beginning of the Great Depression, a time when many religious houses in Vienna sold off their manuscripts, the Yeshiva manuscript was put up for auction.[4] From that time, this manuscript was in a private collection in the United States, until its acquisition by the Yeshiva University Library.

Properly speaking, the YM is not an exact copy of the trial proceedings. Commissioned during the campaign to secure the canonization of "Little Martyr Simon" in Rome, the manuscript includes only selected judicial documents generated by the ritual murder trial. The YM opens with a German translation of Pope Sixtus IV's bull, in order to give the text that follows both a chronological and legitimizing frame. In the words of the author-editor:

> Here, in the first place, is the papal Bull, in which, praise be the diligence and judicial proceedings, our Holy Father the Pope recognizes and declares the duly conducted trial and sentencing against the Jews of Trent, recorded below, on account of the holy, innocent boy named Simon, and that the said trial against the said Jews was conducted in a judicious and upright manner, as one may learn hereafter.[5]

Following the text of the papal bull and the imprint of the coat of arms of the house of Württemberg is the official statement on the trial:

> Now, here following we will begin with every and each aforementioned interrogation and trial, which were carried out in accordance with godly law, against the blasphemers and desecrators of the Passion of Jesus Christ, against the Jews of Trent, on account of the innocent child and holy martyr Simon, who was piteously and inhumanly tortured and murdered by the same Jews; but

first, concerning the accusation and the many great, remarkable, and true signs indicating the aforenamed Jews brought on by the search for the missing child, can be found hereafter.[6]

The next portion of the text constitutes a narrative prologue (fols. 5–17). It provides an official chronology of events between Good Friday and Easter Sunday, taking the reader quickly through a number of scenes: the boy's father, Andreas, approaching the bishop after mass; the search ordered by the podestà, or civil magistrate; the discovery of the corpse in Samuel's house; the examination of the wounds; the conveying of the body to St. Peter's; and the arrests of the first Jews. Written from the simulated perspective of an "eyewitness," this narrative prologue, possibly compiled and edited at a later date than the main body of the text, formed a structurally distinct part of the manuscript, linking the prefatory papal bull with the subsequent judicial text. An authorial voice is clearly present: the narrator, who described and commented on the initial events, was not the law clerk, who simply recorded the subsequent interrogations.

The main body of the YM consists of the trial proceedings. Except for the preliminary examinations of hostile Christian witnesses, who provided some of the "great, remarkable, and true signs indicating the Jews," the main text records the interrogations of nineteen men and four women of the Jewish community in Trent conducted between 28 March 1475 and 6 April 1476 (fols. 24–612). Arranged by witness, the text follows a chronological order within the subsections of the family groups, beginning with the householders and their servants, progressing to their house guests, and concluding with the women. The exception was Samuel, the leader of and spokesman for the Jewish community, whose interrogations were placed first although he was not the first to be questioned by the magistrates. The author-editor explains his arrangement in a passage worth quoting at length in order to give a sense of how the text of the YM was actually put together:

But since the Jews wanted to know or say nothing about these aforementioned remarkable signs and indications, neither about the death or about the wounds of the holy child, Justice commanded, in such a grave matter, that the truth be thoroughly and properly examined through judicial torture, so that such a great evil would not go unpunished, or that anyone innocent might suffer or be suspected on its account. And thus the podestà in Trent himself ordered the Jews to be seized, which he was obliged to do on account of his office, and earnestly examined according to court proceedings, which was proper in such matters. Although the same questions, as recorded in the following trials with the confessions, were first put to Bonaventure, in Italian, or Seligman Jew, as he was named in German, the cook of Samuel Jew; after him to the Other Seligman, son of Mayr Jew; thirdly to Israel, son of Samuel; fourthly to Vital, servant of Samuel; and only in the fifth place to Samuel himself, I began, however, with the same Samuel and dealt with his trial, in view of the fact that he was almost the leader, the instigator and originator of most things, and in my opinion, certain things are said more clearly in his confession.[7]

Who was this "I"? Before attempting an answer, we need to examine more closely the textual and linguistic characteristics of the YM. As I have argued above, the YM is a complex corpus, a compilation and translation of texts from different sources, arranged according to an editorial principle that made it the official story of ritual murder in Trent. Five distinct "voices" can be identified: those of the Christian witnesses, the author-editor, the Jews, the magistrates, and the scribe. The Christian witnesses, including the convert Giovanni, gave damaging testimonies at the beginning of the trial; they occupied a minor role in the YM. The author-editor cannot be identified for certain. Although we do not know the identity of the translator, we do know that the law clerk Hans von Fundo and some of the other witnesses to the interrogations were German speakers who heard first-hand the "confessions" of the Jews, all of whom spoke German. It is a reasonable conjecture that the person who prepared the German text did not depend solely on the written Latin manuscripts but also had access to the vivid memories of the men who had recently seen and heard the Jewish prisoners. Leaving both of these voices aside, we are left with three others. The collective voice of the Jews is actually the different voices of fifteen men and four women, each with its own distinctive history and personality. In the context of the trial, however, they are reduced to one set of interlocutors. The magisterial voice of authority includes the main speaker, the podestà, his colleague the captain, and their interpreters. Also present at the interrogations were jurors, guards, and official witnesses, but they are given only a few lines in the text. The final voice, all-prevailing, belongs to the scribe who recorded the interrogations. There were two such notaries —Hans von Fundo, the official scribe of the criminal court (*Blutschreiber*), who was present during most of the sessions, and Peter Rauter of Maleferrat. Von Fundo asked to be relieved of duty on 28 October 1475 on account of the investigation of the apostolic commissioner, who had accused the authorities in Trent of a miscarriage of justice. The podestà, Giovanni de Salis, refused the request, citing von Fundo's indispensable linguistic skills (he was fluent in German, Italian, and Latin), but agreed to appoint Reuter as a second law clerk.[8] As a rule, the three major voices (magisterial, Jewish, and scribal) are heard indirectly. Sitting in the shadow of the torture chamber, von Fundo usually recorded the dialogue between magistrate and prisoner in the third person; he often resorted to indirect discourse and employed phrases such as *Man fragt,* ("It is asked), a stunning reminder of the ordered procedure and impersonality of judicial torture. Occasionally, direct statements from the prisoners threaten the ordered universe of the transcript, and emotions burst through the bulwark of chancery discourse.

The reader of the manuscript thus is faced with a twofold problem of translation—from speech to text, and from one language to another. The primary instance, the moment of speech, is represented by the dialogues between two sets of interlocutors: the magistrates and the Jews. For setting, we have to imagine the torture chamber in the castle: a bare room, high ceilings, stone walls, a few benches, perhaps a window or two, and the *strappada,* an instrument constructed of a rope and pulley to hoist prisoners. The podestà presided over all sessions; the captain, the city's military commander, was present at many but not all sessions; others—administrators, jurors, and notaries— served as interpreters and official witnesses. Seated at a table supplied with pen, ink, and paper, the scribe described the scene and the dialogue for the record of the court and for posterity. Vivid as the trial record may read, we cannot forget it was written by one man in words alien to the protagonists.

Four languages were actually involved in the interrogations. From the YM, we know that the podestà, Giovanni de Salis of Brescia, was an Italian speaker with a poor command of German; conversely, the captain, Jakob von Sporo, a German, knew little Italian.[9] The interrogation proceeded in this way: The podestà asked questions, in Italian, which one of the interpreters translated into German for the Jews; the answers, in German, were translated back for the podestà; during all this, the scribe tried to write down all that was said, in Latin. Except for the couple Anna and Israel, who were fluent in both German and Italian, the Jews spoke only German; many of them had travelled from central Europe and understood little or no Italian. Twice, in separate interrogations, Israel and Anna gave short answers in Italian—the occasions were remarkable enough that the scribe recorded these speeches in the original. Hebrew came in at two points—when the Jews swore to their confessions and when the magistrates coerced them to repeat the prayers in the Haggadah deemed blasphemous to Christianity. The YM itself registers the polyphony of the trial; it represents a record of multiple translations: from Italian into German, from German back to Italian, from Hebrew into German and Latin, from Italian and German into

Latin, and from the Latin court transcript into the German text of the manuscript. And finally, the manuscript reflects a far more sinister translation—one which transgresses the boundary between fact and fantasy, collapsing voluntary statements into involuntary confessions and distorting Jewish rites into a Christian ethnography of barbarism.[10]

ABBREVIATIONS

AST, APV, C — Archivio di Stato, Trent. Archivio
Principesco-Vescovile, Capsa

SL — Sezione Latina

ST — Sezione Tedesca

ÖNB — Österreichische Nationalbibliothek

"Pro bibliotheca" — *"Pro bibliotheca erigenda": Mostra di
manoscritti ed incunaboli del vescovo di
Trento Iohannes Hinderbach, 1465–1486.*
Trent: Biblioteca comunale, 1989

Processi — *Processi contro gli ebrei di Trento, 1475–
1478.* Vol. 1, *I Processi del 1475.* Ed.
Anna Esposito and Diego Quaglioni.
Padua: CEDAN, 1990

Quaglioni,
Apologia Iudaeorum. — Battista Dei Giudici. *Apologia Iudaeorum.
Invectiva contra Platinam. Propaganda
antiebraica e polemiche di Curia durante il*

Pòntificato di Sisto IV (1471–1484). Ed.
Diego Quaglioni. Rome: Roma nel
Rinascimento, 1987

Rogger   Il Principe Vescovo Giovanni Hinderbach
(1465–1486) fra tardo medioevo e
umanesimo: Incontro di studio, Trento, 2–6
ottobre 1989. Ed. Iginio Rogger. Trent.
N.d., forthcoming.

YM   Yeshiva University Library. New York.
Manuscript record of the trial against
the Jews of Trent ("Prozess gegen die
Juden von Trient")

TRENT 1475

The Yeshiva Manuscript, folio 2v, showing the coat of arms
of the House of Württemberg. Reproduced courtesy of Yeshiva University Library.

CHAPTER ONE

THE PRINCE-BISHOP

Divine service for Good Friday had just concluded. As Johannes Hinderbach walked out of the cathedral, Master Andreas Unferdorben approached "the most reverend prince." He told the bishop that his son Simon had been missing since about the twelfth hour last night, or, "according to the way Germans reckoned time," roughly five in the evening. With the help of friends, Andreas had been looking for his boy, who was not quite two and a half, all over the city and in the neighboring villages. Fearing that Simon might have fallen into a ditch, the search party walked along the canals that led from the Adige River into the city, but they could not find the missing child. The bishop promised help. The podestà ordered his men to spread the news in all quarters of the city: the missing child was last seen wearing a black or grayish-black coat.

Thus began the record of "the trial against the Jewish inhabitants of Trent" as it appears in the Yeshiva manuscript. Compiled in 1478–79, three years after the initial events, this trial record constructed a story from various testimonies, including the Jews' confessions extracted under torture. As a justification of the judicial proceedings, the narrative strove to create order and verisimilitude.[1] It purported to tell of the evil deeds of the Jews by documenting the motives and details of the alleged ritual killing of Simon Unferdorben. But like a badly told story, the Yeshiva manuscript record is full of contradictions and inconsistencies; its claim to historical veracity, founded on an ethnology of anti-Semitism, is subverted by its own grandiose rhetoric. But any attempt to reconstruct the history of the Trent ritual murder trial has to begin with the trial record itself. From the massive tome of this anti-Jewish story, we can isolate narrative fragments, subject these to rigorous textual and historical criticism, and see them in a different pattern. Instead of one story, that of ritual murder, the trial record tells many tales: the fragmentary events in the lives of the imprisoned men and women, remembered under duress; the fabricated murder charge they confessed to under torture; the accusations of Jewhaters, motivated by religious zeal or greed; the charity of Christian neighbors, who secretly offered help to their Jewish neighbors; the legends of Jewish rites and magic, repeated by the simple and the learned; and, finally, of course, the story of the judicially sanctioned executions. Of the many characters who appear in this story, Simon's father begins the tale.

On Saturday 25 March, Andreas came to the podestà again, complaining that nobody had come up with any information on the missing child. "Therefore he petitioned him [the podestà]," in the words of the Yeshiva manuscript, "to send his servants to search the houses of the Jews, and see whether it [the child] could be found because he had heard in many places in the city that during these holy feast days the Jews want to kidnap Christian children secretly and kill them." Andreas continued, "Moreover, someone also advised him to ask the podestà to search the Jewish houses." That "someone" was a man named Zanesus, known simply as *der Schweizer,* the Swiss. As we shall see, der Schweizer was to play a sinister role in the story.

The podestà, Giovanni de Salis, led his men to the house of Samuel, the leader of the Jewish community, and found nothing. The following day, Easter Sunday, March 26, Simon was found dead in Samuel's house. According to the trial record, it was the podestà's men who found the body. A servant, Ulrich, searching with a torch on Sunday evening, found the body in a ditch that flowed into Samuel's house. But that, again, is contradicted by the statements of Samuel, given later during his imprisonment. In fact, it was the Jews who found the child and reported it to the podestà, a crucial detail "uncorrected" in the trial record. When Simon's body was brought before the Jews gathered near the ditch, blood allegedly began to flow. Christians saw this as a divine sign, for they believed that recently murdered victims bled in the presence of their killers. The podestà ordered the corpse to be carried to the Hospital of St. Peter's. His men arrested six Jews: Samuel, Tobias, Engel, Isaac the son of Moses of Bamberg, Joaff, and Seligman. The accused were brought to the Castello del Buonconsiglio, the fortress-like episcopal palace, the seat of the government and the residence of the prince-bishop Johannes Hinderbach.

The blood libel against the Jews of Trent—the accusation that Jews murdered Christians out of religious hatred, often for ritual purposes—was neither the first nor the last in the long series of anti-Jewish charges in European history.[2] Against the broader context of late medieval anti-Semitism, two central themes in the tragedy of 1475 deserve a closer examination. The first may be described as the parallel construction of Christian identities and anti-Jewish images; the second refers to the convergence of anti-Semitism in the actions of secular and ecclesiastical authorities and in the anti-Jewish representations created by the elites and the people.

Beginning in the twelfth century, when the veneration of the Body of Christ was elaborated in new liturgies, devotional practices, and theology, stories of eucharistic abuses also started to circulate.[3] Open to the doubts of skeptics and to the hostility of heretics, the fragile Body of Christ manifested its sacrality precisely in its dialectic of vulnerability and power. Often subject to injuries inflicted by unbelievers, prominent among whom were the Jews, the Host would inevitably triumph in the end by exposing the malefactors to the vengeance or justice of the believers. In these medieval representations of host desecration, depicted in paintings, exempla, chronicles, and plays, the eucharist became interchangeable with the Christ Child, thus revealing the intimate morphology between the discourses of eucharistic abuse, Christian sacrifice, and ritual murder.[4] Although these purported blasphemies were widely ascribed to Jews, they could be projected onto any group that threatened the ecclesiastical order.[5] Images of child murder, conjurations of black magic, and the specter of cannibalistic rituals informed the rich polemical language of the official Church writings that could be applied to heretics, Jews, and witches.

Take the example of San Bernardino of Siena. He preached in the summer of 1427 against a secret sect of heretics and witches in the Piedmont who had allegedly murdered five inquisitors sent to investigate them. According to the friar, at a certain time every year the heretics would abduct a little boy and throw him from hand to hand until he died. They then pulverized the body and put the powder in a cup from which they all drank.[6] With minor variations, the motifs in Bernardino's sermon would emerge in blood libels against Jews, specifically in the record of the 1475 Trent trial, as well as in descriptions of the witches' sabbath. Only six years separated the conclusion of the Trent affair in Rome and the promulgation of Innocent VIII's 1484 papal bull against witchcraft.

In addition to the intimate dialectic between medieval Christian piety and anti-Semitism, individual cases of persecution of

Jews must also be understood in historical context. The most significant development of the fourteenth and fifteenth centuries was the cooperation of different social groups in common actions against the Jews. A period of profound crisis, the late Middle Ages saw the convergence of ecclesiastical, secular, and popular anti-Semitism, a development conclusively demonstrated by František Graus in his study of the Black Death and the destruction of Jewish communities.[7] The massacres of Jews during the period 1348–50, concurrent with the plague, established the pattern of persecutions for the next hundred and fifty years. Religious hatred and economic resentment created a powerful force that destroyed Jewish communities and coerced conversions to Christianity. In its longstanding polemic against the synagogue, the Church furnished the theological arguments against the Jews, the "killers of Christ"; in the violent attacks on usury, preached by the mendicant orders, religious fervor fueled economic grievances against Jewish moneylenders. For secular authorities, judicial polemics joined the arsenal of theological anti-Semitism; during political crises, it often became easier for ruling elites to initiate persecutions or simply yield to the popular fury that demanded the sacrifice of Jewish scapegoats.

In territories where secular and ecclesiastical jurisdictions were combined in the authority of a single person, the prince-bishop, the full weight of official repression could be brought down swiftly upon religious minorities. Trent was one of these ecclesiastical principalities of the Holy Roman Empire.

"The most reverend and dignified Lord Johannes, by the Grace of God and the Apostolic See Bishop and Lord of Trent" was the fourth bishop by that name.[8] Born on 14 August 1418, in the vicinity of Rauschenberg just outside Kassel in Hesse, Johannes Hinderbach belonged to the first generation of northern humanists. His father, also named Johannes, served as a juror in Rauschenberg, near Marburg; his mother, Immeln (Emeludis) von Langenstein, was the great-niece of Heinrich von Langenstein,

Figure 1. Johannes Hinderbach. From *Madonna with Saints* by Girolomo da Trento, late fifteenth-century painting. Reproduced courtesy of Museo Diocesano Tridentino.

the famous theologian at the University of Vienna. The sixteen-year-old Johannes enrolled at the university: in 1436 he obtained the baccalaureate, two years later the master of arts. Having begun legal studies, in 1440 Hinderbach, like generations of German students before and after him, enrolled in the faculty of law in Padua; ten years later, he attained the distinction of doctor of canon law. A friend of Aeneas Silvius Piccolomini, he resembled in many ways his more famous contemporary who was a noted humanist, Imperial secretary, canon of the Trent cathedral chapter (1431–1439), and ultimately Pope Pius II. Hinderbach was also an imperial servant who attained ecclesiastical honors through loyalty to the Habsburgs.[9]

Hinderbach entered imperial service in 1449 as a secretary to Friedrich III; as a reward for his diplomatic service in Milan, the emperor granted him the benefice at Mödling parish near Vienna. More rewards came Hinderbach's way. In 1453 he followed the emperor to Rome. The same year, Pope Calixus III granted him a benefice in Trent, in exchange for which Hinderbach resigned his benefice at St. Stefan's in Vienna. Over the next several years, the noble coucillor received other missions and honors: in 1458, when his friend Aeneas Silvius was elected pope in Siena, Friedrich sent Hinderbach to extend imperial congratulations; in 1459, the emperor bestowed on Hinderbach the title Count Palatine Laterano of the Holy Roman Empire; between 1461 and 1462, he was sent on an imperial mission to Bohemia; a year later, he represented Friedrich in rendering obedience to the new pope, Paul II.

Between Rome and Vienna, the respective seats of papacy and empire, Hinderbach traveled the path of success. Serving as the imperial legate in Rome, he was elected in 1465 by the cathedral chapter in Trent to be the new bishop. Hinderbach could not assume his ecclesiastical post immediately; on 20 July 1466 he was confirmed and consecrated in Rome. Following his triumphal entry into Trent, Hinderbach received the imperial investiture from his old master, Friedrich III.

Halfway between Vienna and Rome, the principality of Trent was the southernmost territory of the Holy Roman Empire. Nominally an imperial fief (hence the imperial investiture for Hinderbach), Trent lay at the crossroads between the Germanic and Italian worlds. In the fifteenth century, the southern Tirol was the scene of a vigorous population expansion. Migrating from the crowded highlands, German-speaking farmers and miners settled gradually toward the foothills and valleys of the south. At the midpoint of the north-south passage, Trent absorbed many German immigrants. During the late fifteenth and sixteenth century, as many as one-quarter of the population might have been German-speakers.[10] While some Trentini were bilingual, the Italian and German communities kept to themselves. In spite of the Italian majority and distinctly north-Italian civic institutions, as in the office of the podestà for example, German travelers of the late fifteenth century considered Trent the beginning of *Germania,* as they left the plains around Verona for the journey home through the mountains of central Europe.[11]

Trent was thus ideally located for Hinderbach the imperial diplomat. The responsibilities of the bishopric did not seem to have slowed down his travels: in 1469 he served as imperial ambassador in Rome; in 1471, he presided as an imperial legate at the Diet of Regensburg; in 1474, he attended the Diet of Augsburg.

Between diplomacy and ecclesiastic office, Hinderbach eagerly pursued his interest in the arts and in the *studia humanitatis.* An avid collector of manuscripts, a friend and correspondent of northern Italian humanists, supporter of Franciscan preachers, and an able administrator, Hinderbach seemed to exemplify the unity of action and learning so lauded in humanist rhetoric. But who was the man behind the ecclesiastical dignities, the self expressed in various representations? Who was Johannes Hinderbach?

Unlike his friend Aeneas Silvius, who bequeathed to posterity a vivid portrait of his amorous and intellectual exploits before his election as pope, Hinderbach, in taciturn Germanic fashion, revealed little about his self. He left clues, nevertheless, in letters, marginal notations in books, and the like. Two things, it seems, mattered to him: power and piety.

For a man of his status and learning, success was measured by advancement in the ecclesiastical hierarchy. By the time of his episcopal election as bishop, Hinderbach had already far surpassed the achievements of his father. Could he have advanced to the papal curia? The tiara was, perhaps, far beyond his reach; after the Schism that ultimate glory seemed reserved for Italian churchmen, and aristocratic ones at that. If Hinderbach could not hope to emulate Aeneas Silvius, it was entirely reasonable to compare himself with his fellow countryman Nicolaus of Kues, known as Cusanus (1401–64). Was not Cusanus, like himself, an imperial and papal servant, a learned and pious churchman? Cusanus served as the bishop of Brixen, just to the north of Trent, and was elevated to the College of Cardinals. Whatever ambitions Hinderbach might have nurtured in private, his standing at the Habsburg court diminished after 1467, with the death of Empress Eleonora. The relationship between Hinderbach and Friedrich III slowly deteriorated; the emperor explicitly forbade his servant to secure the cardinal's hat.[12] By the time of his election to the bishopric of Trent, Hinderbach had lost the political support he had formerly enjoyed in Vienna.

Trent offered moderate rewards to offset the loss of imperial patronage. Unlike Italian bishoprics (with the notable exception of Rome), the diocese was similar to German bishoprics in structure, uniting both secular and spiritual jurisdictions. Trent was a principality governed by the bishop with the counsel of ecclesiastical noblemen, the canons of the cathedral chapter. The statutes of the fifteenth and sixteenth centuries stipulated that two thirds were to be selected from German noble families, one third from Italian families.[13] As the titular head of the secular and ecclesiastical authorities in the territory, the prince-bishop found his power strictly circumscribed by the Habsburgs. After his election, Hinderbach had to renew the compact which bound his predecessor, Georg Hack, to Archduke Sigismund of Tirol. The compact required an oath of fealty from Hinderbach, who also had to accept from Sigismund the appointment of a captain, the keeper of the city key and military commander in Trent.[14] During his entire episcopate, Hinderbach kept a vigilant eye on Sigismund, who was intent on extending his jurisdiction over the prince-bishops of Brixen and Trent.[15]

For Hinderbach, religion was not merely a career; the glory of episcopal office demanded a proper disposition. Hinderbach remembered his illustrious kinsman, Heinrich von Langenstein, whose piety and learning secured his reputation. The young Hinderbach, enrolled at the University of Vienna, must have heard legends of the brilliant professor, who dominated the faculty of theology during the 1390s. Among Hinderbach's collection of manuscripts and incunabula were two manuscripts by Langenstein: "The Exposition on the Canon of the Mass"[16] and "Commentaries on Genesis."[17] On the opening folio of volume one of the "Commentaries," Hinderbach drew a family genealogy, linking himself to Langenstein. In another manuscript Hinderbach wrote margin notes on his relationship to the great scholar. The work "History of Emperor Friedrich III", composed by his humanist friend Aeneas Silvius, praised the intellectual excitement at the University of Vienna, established by the emperor: "There is a school of liberal arts, of theology, and of Canon Law, recently authorized by the pope. A large number of students congregate here, from Hungary and South Germany. There are two famous and outstanding theologians: Heinrich of Hesse, educated in Paris, who hastened hither at the commencement of the university, who occupied the first professorship, and composed many remarkable volumes." In his own hand, Hinderbach made a notation above "Heinrich of Hesse," and at the bottom of the folio he added: "Master Heinrich of Hesse: he was from the lineage of my mother, who was born of my grandmother, who was the daughter of his sister of the village Langenstein."[18] Hinderbach, proud of his lineage, obviously believed that he was also destined to achieve great fame.[19]

To understand Hinderbach is to understand a great deal about the religious and political context of the trial of 1475. Christian piety, buttressed by learning, was not meek or humble; Christian doctrine was power incarnate: it exposed, ridiculed, and crushed the enemies of the Church. If the power of Christian piety was demonstrated during the ritual murder trial of 1475, its significance, for Hinderbach, stretched back further in his experience. To understand the events of 1475 and after we have to remember

Hinderbach's formative years: his student days, his illustrious kinsman Langenstein, and the university, Jewish community, and city of Vienna.

With a population of approximately fifteen thousand at the end of the fifteenth century, Vienna, the capital of the Habsburg empire, was a mere shadow of the great European cities of the day. The imperial court, one-tenth of the population, clearly dominated the city. The Jewish community, although smaller in size than that of Prague, was one of the largest in central Europe; the Jewish quarter, walled off and accessible only through four gates, consisted of sixty-nine buildings and five hundred inhabitants.[20]

One of the luminaries appointed to the new university at Vienna was the theologian Heinrich von Langenstein, who left a post in Oxford for his German-speaking native land. Educated in Paris, strongly influenced by the Thomist synthesis of natural philosophy and theology, Langenstein would come to reject Aristotelian logic in matters of faith. This turn of mind came about during the 1390s, as a result of his encounter with the Jewish community of Vienna.

In Paris, Langenstein had studied Hebrew with Jewish converts. During the Great Schism (1378–1415), Langenstein demonstrated a keen interest in the prophecies of Hildegard of Bingen and Joachim of Fiore, and in the conversion of Jews. Numerous references to Jews are scattered in his writings; he also wrote two works that dealt extensively with aspects of Jewish life and culture: "On the Hebrew idioms" (1388) and "Treatise on Contracts" (1390–91).[21] He argued fervently against usury and vented his anger at the mingling of Jews and Christians.

In Vienna, Langenstein probably had personal contacts with the Jewish community; he might have conversed with its leading resident and visiting scholars—Rabbi Meir ben Baruch Halevi, Abraham Klausner, and Rabbi Yom Tov Lipmann Mühlhausen, composer of the "Sefer ha-Nizzahon." One can imagine him trying to demonstrate to the rabbis the errors of their faith and almost hear their response, their insistence on decisive logical argumentation or Scriptural evidence to demonstrate the truth of Christianity.[22] Whatever contacts he might have established, Langenstein reached the following conclusion in 1396. On 25 November, the feast day of St. Catherine of Alexandria, the patron saint of the faculty of arts, Langenstein preached a sermon to the university community:

> First of all, the infidel must be willing to acquiesce in the probable and persuasive reasons possible in moral matters, reasons that ought to move any rational man. He must concede this if he is a rational man, since demonstrating certainty should not be sought in all matters, least of all in moral matters. . . . If the infidel does not concede this assumption, then he is obstinate even in the sciences of the infidels; therefore, he cannot be persuaded by the path of reason. And this is why the Jews cannot be persuaded by arguments, because they are stubborn.[23]

Langenstein saw the Jews as deprived of reason, cut off from the Sign of salvation, the *Verbum Dei,* and, by implication, an irrational, superstitious, and obstinate people. Their language, incapable of sustaining rational discourse, could only function on the level of magical symbols. Langenstein died one year later but his writings created an anti-Jewish milieu at the University of Vienna for the generations that followed.

The crisis of authority of the medieval Church came to a head with Jan Hus, the Prague professor burnt at the Council of Constance for his critique of the Roman Church. In the subsequent Hussite uprising (1415–1436), religious and nationalist movements created a new order in Bohemia. Inspired by the coming millennium and the rule of the just, prophesied in Revelation, radical followers of Hus established a mountain stronghold at Tabor, creating a self-conscious community of the "elect." The Hussite revolution sent a wave of excitement through the Jewish communities of central Europe; the disintegration of the Church signified, it seemed, the coming of the long-awaited Messiah. Hus was honored as God's witness in Jewish writings; Rabbi Abigdor

Kara of Prague composed a hymn in Hebrew and Yiddish to praise the shared messianism of the Hussites and Jews.[24]

The Catholic reaction came swiftly. In 1419, a charge was raised at the University of Vienna, accusing Jews, Hussites, and Waldensians of conspiring to overthrow the Roman Church. On 1 March 1420, Pope Martin V declared a crusade against the Hussites. At Easter, some Viennese Jews were accused of desecration of the Host; they were arrested and imprisoned. Nicolaus of Dinkelsbühl, theologian and disciple of Langenstein, urged forced conversions upon the entire Jewish community. On 12 March 1421, some 240 persons of the Jewish community who refused baptism were burned at the stake. The Jewish quarter was abolished, and the university received as gifts, the books and properties confiscated from the martyred Jews.[25]

Some years later, in 1464, when Hinderbach had achieved some prominence, he received a prognosticon, published in Padua and entitled *Antichrist of the Jews,* a proclamation of the imminent advent of a Jewish Antichrist.[26] It is not clear whether or not Hinderbach ever had personal contact with Jews. Suffice to say that he was very much shaped by a culture and a historical era, which castigated Jews as the quintessential internal enemies of Christians, an image nurtured by the presence of small but widespread Jewish communities in Christian lands, including Hinderbach's own principality of Trent.

CHAPTER TWO

THE JEWISH COMMUNITY

Apart from the trial proceedings, almost no sources document the conditions of the small Jewish community in Trent, which consisted of three households. Yet the trial record, with its extensive transcription and translation of the prisoners' verbal statements, has preserved for posterity the voices of the men and women of that community. And from the stories they told about themselves, of the humdrum daily routine and the drama of persecution, we can imagine their world before it was shattered and see, however fleetingly, a picture of their lives.

Divided into three households, the Jewish community in Trent consisted of the family groups of Samuel, Tobias, and Engel. The majority of the Jews were recent immigrants from German-speaking central Europe, where a wave of expulsions and persecutions drove many to seek refugee in Italy.[1] Each of the families was headed by a male householder, who presided over an extended

kin group and publicly represented the family in the larger Christian community: the householders subscribed to the letters of
protection granted by the authorities; they paid annual tributes;
they represented their kin in legal proceedings; and they were
generally responsible for the conduct of their "housefolk." As was
the custom of the Ashkenazim, each Jewish household in Trent
gathered under one roof a core agnatic kin group that ranged up
to five generations.[2] In addition to blood relatives, the households
also included people who passed in and out of the families' lives.
Some were servants whose loyalty stretched back more than a
dozen years; others were rabbinic students and scribes temporarily employed by the households; and still others were poor wandering Jews who enjoyed the families' hospitality en route between central Europe and Italy.

Samuel headed the largest of the three households in Trent. In
1475 Samuel's household consisted of eleven people, ten adults
and a child, living in a spacious house. The oldest member, Moses,
was eighty years of age; the next generation consisted of two
middle-age couples (Samuel, forty-five, Brünnlein, forty, Mayer,
forty, and Schönlein, thirty-six); the next generation included
Israel (twenty-five), Anna (twenty-three), and Seligman (between
nineteen and twenty); the youngest was Anna's child, a mere
toddler. In addition to family members there were two German-
speaking servants: Vital, son of Seligman of Weissenburg, and
Seligman the cook (also called by his Italian name Bonaventure),
the son of Samuel of Nuremberg.

The son of Seligman of Nuremberg, Samuel was born probably
around 1430 to a comfortable if not well-off family that gave him
a traditional education in Hebrew. During his interrogation in
1475, Samuel recalled that he had studied with Rabbi David
Sprintz in Bamberg and Nuremberg around 1445.[3] Like many of
his coreligionists, Samuel left central Europe for Italy, perhaps to
escape persecutions, or to seek a better living. He settled in Trent
in 1461.[4] Although Samuel and his wife changed their names,
Samuel (formerly Schallman) and Brünnlein (in Italian, Brunetta)

retained much of their past.[5] The scribe at the Trent interrogations recorded that Samuel answered in German, not Italian, a language he spoke poorly. It seems that Samuel's household was bilingual: the three oldest generations spoke Yiddish; the fourth generation was functionally bilingual, except for Anna, Samuel's daughter-in-law, who spoke Italian; and their child probably learned both languages. Samuel's lineage represented a family in cultural transition: through his daughter-in-law, Anna, the family established connections with the important Jewish communities of the Venetian Republic; between Israel and Anna, Italian was the language of daily life and affection. The other lineage residing in the household was decidedly German.

A moneylender by profession, Samuel and his household lived in Trent under the protection of the prince-bishop, a privilege renewed in 1469 by Johannes Hinderbach, who had been elected to the see four years earlier. In exchange for a "Jewish tax," payable annually at Christmas, Hinderbach accepted in his grace and protection "Samuel Jew residing here in Trent, together with his wife, children, servants, and housefolk." The privilege, contracted for five years, granted the Jews residence in Trent, the right of travel in the territory, and permission to set up a money-lending and pawnbroking business.[6]

Samuel's was by no means the first Jewish household in Trent. In 1403, Bishop Ulrich III of Brixen granted to a certain Isaac and his family a privilege to reside in Brixen and lend money in Bolzano and Trent. The first direct evidence of a Jewish presence in Trent, however, dates from 1440: on 3 September Bishop Alessandro condemned Peter of Rido to pay interest to Isaac for money owed. Ten years later, Sigismund, now Count of Tirol, who claimed Trent as his fief, conceded to "Elias and other Jewish men and women of ours in Trent. . . the enjoyment of. . . all the rights and statues. . . as the citizens of the same [city]."[7] We do not know whether or not Samuel was related to Isaac or Elias, but the Jewish presence in Trent, after scarcely more than a generation, had provoked suspicion and hostility from the beginning: these memories would resurface during the 1475 blood libel.

Two lineages of the same agnatic group lived in Samuel's house. The main lineage, headed by Samuel, consisted of three generations: Samuel himself and Brünnlein, their son Israel and his wife Anna, and an infant grandchild. We know very little about Brünnlein—she is hardly mentioned in the trial record—but her daughter-in-law, Anna, gave vivid testimony of her own life. Born in 1452, the daughter of Abraham of Brescia, Anna grew up in Montagna near Padua. She lived with her father for seventeen years, where she learned to read Italian and Hebrew.[8] In 1469 Anna married Israel, probably in Montagna; after one year, the couple moved to Trent.[9] Soon, the young bride gave birth (the documents do not mention the sex of the child), an occasion that planted the seeds of tragedy. During Anna's labor, Samuel employed a Christian midwife, Dorothea. Her husband, Zanesus, also known as the Schweizer, quarreled with Samuel and Israel over Dorothea's fee. The Schweizer filed a lawsuit, was unhappy with the judgment award of two pounds, and pestered Samuel into offering him more. Finally, Samuel gave him four pounds. Thereafter they were enemies and over the next few years the Schweizer often threatened Samuel. Although the Schweizer got his way, he apparently nurtured a deep resentment.[10]

Although Samuel was the householder and the patriarch, he was not the oldest member of the family. That honor belonged to Moses of Franconia, "the Old One," who had reached the venerable age of eighty in 1475.[11] In all likelihood he was Samuel's uncle.

The sources do not tell us the exact relationship between the two lineages, but we can establish probable kinship ties based on age comparisons and anecdotal information. Israel and "the Other Seligman" were described as cousins; their fathers, Samuel and Mayer, belonged to the same generation and were probably cousins as well. From Moses' confessions, we catch a few glimpses of his life: forty years earlier, in about 1435) he was in Würzburg; by 1445 he lived in Speyer; in 1460, he settled in the Tirol (Hall and Mül). In 1465, he moved yet again, for the last time, to Trent.[12] In 1465, Moses had moved to Trent,[13] accompanied by his son, Mayer of Nuremberg, his daughter-in-law, Schönlein (in Italian, Bella), and his grandson, Seligman (called "the Other Seligman" or "Seligman the German" in the trial record).[14]

With the exception of Moses, this second lineage was somewhat younger than Samuel's lineage. Mayer and Schönlein married in 1455 in Hall; she was sixteen at the time, and he was most likely only a few years older.[15] Their son, Seligman, described in the trial record as between eighteen and twenty-five, must have been born in 1455 or 1456.[16] Whatever reasons brought them to Trent, Moses and this second lineage were dependent on Samuel, the householder and head of the family business.

Used for multiple functions, the house consisted of three spatial divisions: private quarters for household members; public space where Samuel talked business, loaned money, and redeemed pledges; and areas for the Jewish community including a hall that served as the synagogue and a water cellar that served as the ritual bath for the women. The trial record gives us a detailed description of the synagogue. Leading into the "schül" was a small antechamber reserved for the women; the entrance faced onto the almemor in the middle where the Torah scroll was read during services; beyond the almemor was space reserved for the men of Samuel's household; to the left of the entrance Engel's menfolk would have stood, to the right, Tobias' household; under the window on the west side of the synagogue was space designated for traveling pious Jews.[17]

Tobias of Magdeburg, a physician by profession, headed another household of six adults and four children. The son of Jordan of Wardburg in Saxony, Tobias arrived in Trent in 1462, one year after Samuel.[18] An eye specialist, Tobias succeeded in building a reputation for himself through thirteen years of medical practice among the Christians of Trent. His first marriage to a woman named Anna seems to have been a fruitful one. Together they raised four sons, of whom Moses, apparently the oldest, had been sent away to school by 1475, leaving his younger brothers, Josche, Haym, and David, aged eight to ten, at home. In 1474, Tobias lost his wife to illness. He married again, in January 1475. He was probably in his late thirties.[19]

His second wife, Sara, was the daughter of Abraham of Schwäbisch Werd. She spoke German, like Tobias, and did not know Italian but could read Hebrew.[20] Considerably younger than her husband (she was twenty-five when she married Tobias), Sara had also lost a spouse. As a girl of thirteen or fourteen, she had been married off by her father to a man named Helas and lived with him in Marburg for six years. One year after his death, she and her daughter, Norhella, moved to "Maysters in teruiser Land" (the Tirol). Four years later she met and married Tobias.[21] In addition to her domestic tasks, Sara would had to take care of the four children, all within a couple of years in age.

Tobias had engaged a tutor to teach his sons. Moses "the Schoolmaster," son of Salomon of Ansbach, was a young man between nineteen and twenty years of age at the time of the trial.[22] Born in the village of Rücklingen, "two German miles" from Ansbach, Moses had to fend for himself early in life.[23] He spent ten years of his youth in Nuremberg, lodging first with a Moses Laff for eight years and then with Joshua for six months. During seven of the Nuremberg years, by Moses' own admission, he lived from the charity of the Jewish hospital.[24] Yet somehow, Moses learned Hebrew and the scriptures. He came to Trent during Passover in 1475 and accepted Tobias' offer: he would tutor the boys for six months in exchange for room and board and two ducats.[25] It is likely that Tobias also found the young man useful to himself; just before their arrests, Moses and Tobias were in the study reading a guide for Jewish housefathers on the governance of their housefolk.[26]

Three other men sealed their fate with Tobias that Passover: Salomon, son of Mendlein and formerly of Innsbruck, served as the family cook,[27] whereas Joaff and Israel, father and son, were celebrating the holiday in Trent en route from Lombardy to Germany.[28] A relative of Tobias, Joaff was the son of Seligman of Ansbach. He turned out to be the proverbial poor cousin, turning up in Trent with his son, Israel, on 23 March. Tobias gave Joaff three or four ducats.[29] On account of his poverty, the trial record described Joaff as Tobias' servant.[30] Joaff was a poor rural Jew from Franconia. Married with children, he served Mayer of Würzburg for sixteen years before he was able to save enough to purchase a horse and wagon. Working for himself, Joaff earned a living transporting merchant goods around Ansbach. In his own words, he had never learned Hebrew, a man who "did not know the prayers and blessings and could only drive a wagon."[31] Tragically for Joaff and Israel, they shared the fate of their host.

The third household was headed by Engel. A recent immigrant, Engel moved to Trent in 1471 from the "Castle Gauardn" (Gavardo) near Brixen, where he had lived with an uncle for seven years.[32] His parents, Salomon and Brünnlein of Bern, raised two children, Engel and Gütlein (also called Bona in the trial record).[33] Fragments of the family history can be reconstructed from Gütlein's testimonies at the 1475 trial. Their father died when Gütlein was thirteen or fourteen; the year was probably 1453 or 1454, judging from the later dates of events in her life. Their widowed mother, Brünnlein, married a man named Hayim who lived in Friaul in Kuniglan, taking her children to the new household. [34]

After nine years in Kuniglan, the grown children went their separate ways. Engel, probably in his early twenties and saddled with the responsibility of his wife Süsslein and a newborn son, struck out on his own; we find him a few years later, in 1464, living with his uncle, most likely as a junior business associate. Business thrived, and a second son was born in 1467.[35]

Gütlein also left Kuniglan. Around 1462 she married a man named Hayim; they lived for three years in Maners (which she described as sixteen miles from Monar), where she bore three sons. Addicted to gambling, Hayim squandered the family possessions and abandoned Gütlein. Unable to provide for her family, Gütlein returned to her mother in Kuniglan. Hayim found her there and wanted her to come back; she refused. In 1469 she obtained a divorce from him.[36]

In 1471, Engel established his own business in Trent. A financially secure man in his thirties, Engel was ready to play the role of patriarch, cherishing, perhaps, the memory of his late father: he would take care of the women of his family, his twice-widowed mother and divorced sister, as well as his wife and children. Within a few years of his arrival, Engel could afford to employ two servants: Lazarus, his nephew and son of Aaron of Seravall, a young man from Friaul;[37] and Isaac, "son of Jacob the Jew from Gridel near Vedera," an immigrant from Voitsberg near Cleburg who had been a schoolboy in Worms in 1460.[38]

At the time of the murder accusation, six adults and three children comprised the Engel household: Engel himself, Süsslein, their two sons, Salomon and Moses (aged fifteen and eight), his mother Brünnlein, most likely in her fifties, his sister Gütlein, and his ten-year-old nephew Salomon, the youngest of Gütlein's three sons and perhaps her only child to survive infancy, and his two servants.

In the eyes of the other two Jewish families, Engel and his kin seemed like parvenus. During the interrogations, testimonies revealed tensions that had existed in the small Jewish community. Although accepted by the other well-established Jewish households, Engel's was a step down the social ladder. Unlike Samuel and Tobias, Engel never mentioned extensive Hebrew study; in fact, his sister, Gütlein, admitted ignorance of Hebrew, unlike Sarah and Anna, who could read the language, and Schönlein, who could write Yiddish. Their servants also disliked one another; under the pressure of torture, as we shall see, they tried to pin blame of the alleged murder on the other households. One significant detail: Engel's household, like Samuel's, had also once retained the services of Dorothea, the Schweizer's wife; and similarly, there was a dispute.[39]

Nevertheless the three families gathered to celebrate Passover yet once again, in memory of the deliverance of the Jews from Egypt, in the hope of their own deliverance to come. Joining the Trent community in their service were several traveling Jews— friends, relatives, or strangers to whom the families offered hospitality. Standing under the west window of the synagogue during Passover, behind members of the three Trent households, the visitors, Moses and Lazarus (both known as "the Pious"), David, Israel the painter, and Moses of Bamberg and his son Isaac, all German Jews, joined in prayer. The first three left Trent immediately after Passover; Israel, Moses, and Isaac stayed a few days longer and were arrested with their hosts.[40]

Israel the painter, twenty-three years of age, son of Mayer of Brandenburg, arrived in Trent on the Saturday before Palm Sunday. Returning from northern Italy, Israel was on his way to Passau when he accepted Samuel's hospitality Saturday night. The next day, Palm Sunday, he left and got as far as Bozen before he hurt his left foot. Unable to purchase a horse, he had to interrupt his journey. While visiting a patient in Bozen, Tobias ran into Israel and invited him to spend Passover in Trent while he recovered from his injury.[41] We can imagine Israel gladly accepting this generous offer. Little did he know that he would play a leading role in the trial. During his subsequent stay in Trent, not a week but eleven months, Israel would have many moments to reproach his bitter fate in Bozen. He gave the longest and most detailed testimonies, and yet he remained an enigmatic figure in this drama.

The unfortunate Moses of Bamberg and Isaac, father and son, were on their way from Bayreuth to Padua. A poor but pious man, Moses wanted to leave his son with a relative in Padua before returning to Germany.[42] During their stopover in Trent, Moses stayed with Samuel while his son lodged in Engel's house.[43] The

Figure 2. Celebration of the Seder, detail from the *Haggadah* of the "Rothschild Miscellany," folio 106b. Text from the *Hilkhot Hamezu-Mazzah*, excerpted from Maimonides' *Mishneh Torah*. Illuminated manuscript, northern Italy, ca. 1470. Reproduced courtesy of the Israel Museum, Jerusalem.

son of Aaron of Ansbach, Moses had seen better days. Twelve years earlier, in 1463, Moses had had his own household in the village of Hechelshaim, six "German" miles from Bayreuth. He had been schooled in Hebrew, and the family had a maid named Gottle.[44] In 1467 his wife, Freyd, died and things began to fall apart. Shattered by her death, Moses led a wandering life, working here and there for wages: six months in Ulm, five years in Heydenfels (Franconia), six months with a certain Mayer, nine months with Leo his own son in the "Castle Spervall," and six months in the little town of St. Johannis "in Plarentmer Gegent."[45] In preparation for the trip to Padua, easily a month's journey from Bayreuth, Moses obtained a letter from Rabbi Moses of Nuremberg, certifying him as a poor pious Jew deserving of alms.[46] Thus equipped, Moses and Isaac made their way to Trent, thanks to the hospitality of the Jewish communities en route.

The Jewish families of Trent lived in a German-speaking neighborhood located near the city wall, close to the Adige River, not far from the Castello del Buonconsiglio. Samuel and Tobias, in fact, were next-door neighbors, while Engel's home was a few houses away. In a densely populated neighborhood, with contiguous houses, narrow streets, and open ditches, the Jews were in daily contact with their Christian neighbors.[47] From windows and doors, one saw people coming and going; from the street, one heard domestic noises and voices; and through openings in common walls, neighbors could talk to one another.

As moneylenders, Samuel and Engel received customers in their houses, taking pawns, making loans, and redeeming pledges. As a physician, Tobias visited many Christian patients at home to prescribe cures and medicine.[48] All three families also occasionally hired Christian help: the midwife Dorothea, married to Johannes "the Schweizer," a sharecropper; the gravedigger, Old Johannes; and Roper, better known in the neighborhood as the Jews' tailor. There were allies and foes among the Christians. As we have seen, the Schweizer was no friend. However, Roper,

Samuel's next door neighbor, was a friend, who came to visit and play cards. Anna, the wife of Roper's cousin Bertold, also seemed to have been a friend of Samuel's household.

On seemingly intimate terms with their Christian neighbors, the Jewish families remained outsiders in the neighborhood, for their religion and occupation set them apart. Although there are no tax records extant, it is obvious that the Jewish families stood out with their wealth and apparent leisure in a community of artisans and sharecroppers, a neighborhood inhabited also by the tanner Andreas Unferdorben, his wife Maria, and their children, among them little Simon.

Passover 5235 might not have been of particular significance for the Jewish families of Trent, but Easter 1475 was special for the town's Christians. The well-known Franciscan preacher, Bernardino da Feltre, came to Trent to deliver the Lenten sermons, in which he lacerated the Jews for practicing usury and chided Christians for associating with them. He foretold an evil that would soon befall the city.[49]

CHAPTER THREE

THE INQUEST

Ⅰt was almost supper time on 26
March 1475 (Easter Sunday), and Samuel's house was bustling
with activity. The men of the community—Samuel, his son Israel,
Tobias, and Engel—were praying in the synagogue. Brünnlein,
the mistress of the household, was in the kitchen overseeing the
preparation of dinner.[1] Her daughter-in-law, Anna, had been sick
for weeks and was lying in bed in her room.[2] Brünnlein sent the
cook, Seligman, down to the cellar to fetch water. Connected to
an outside ditch, the cellar, where water was stored, also served as
the monthly ritual bath for the women. As recently as the previous Thursday, Passover, Sara had taken a ritual bath; with
her were Brünnlein and a Christian woman, Anna, the wife of
Bertold.[3]

In the cellar, Seligman saw something in the water. To his
horror, he recognized the body of a small boy. He hurried back to
the kitchen, reported what he saw to Brünnlein, and the two

headed for the synagogue. The four men had just finished their prayers and were walking out the door. When they heard Brünnlein's story, they knew the body had to be Simon's. For a couple of days, rumor had been circulating around Trent suggesting that the Jews were responsible for Simon's disappearance. After the podestà had searched Samuel's house on Friday, the Jews discussed ways to avoid the evil that might befall them if someone threw a dead child into one of their houses.[4] Engel's household, which had settled in Trent only four years earlier, seemed particularly unnerved by the accusations. On Good Friday, 24 March, Süsslein told Isaac the cook of the great outcry among the Christians on account of the missing child.[5] Immediately, Engel ordered Isaac to check his cellar; still anxious the next day, he told Isaac to close the windows there so that no one could throw a dead child into the cellar.[6]

The men took counsel. They thought some Christians must have killed the boy, thrown his body into the ditch, and let the water carry it into Samuel's cellar. Tobias' advice was that they report the dead child to the authorities. Perhaps trying to reassure everyone, Samuel said he was glad the body was found; now, the matter would come to a close. It was resolved that the three householders would go to the podestà to report the discovery.[7] Tobias first went home to tell Sara the bad news. She had just finished cooking and asked him whether he wanted dinner. Tobias said he would first go to the podestà and report on the missing child.[8] Together, the three men set out for the Buonconsiglio, only a short walk away.

The Jews had little choice. Living under official toleration, they were completely dependent on the good will of the authorities for their livelihood and legal status. Fear, not trust, induced deference to authority. At the castle, the three men offered the guard one gulden not to detain them.[9] Released by the podestà after making their report, they hurried home.

While the men were away making their report, the three households were in turmoil. At Tobias' house, Sara fed the children and then asked their tutor Moses to help pack away the family silver in a sack.[10] In a brief moment, her whole world had turned upside down. Only a few hours before, after their day's meal, she was happily playing cards in her home with the other Jewish women and Old Moses' grandson, Seligman.[11] Now, everybody was worried about being arrested. A mother herself, Sara felt sad because the boy had drowned; she was more worried that her husband would be arrested at the castle.[12] Tobias returned after half an hour, quite agitated. The cook, Salomon, went into Tobias' room and said: "I don't believe that we Jews do such things." Tobias exploded: "Don't be my spokesman! You should not say that you believe Jews do not do such things. You should forswear, they never do it!"[13] Both Israel and Moses, Tobias' employees and house guests, wanted to flee, but the patriarch forbade it. Tobias then went over to Samuel's house and told him of the panic; Samuel, still trusting in the authorities, admonished that if anyone fled, all Jews would come under suspicion.[14]

A group went down to Samuel's cellar that Sunday evening. As the physician, Tobias took charge. He asked "the Other Seligman" to light the way with a candle and told Joaff to fish the body out of the water.[15] Apparently Tobias had time to examine the body. Later, during his interrogation, he would repeat his observations: the boy, according to Tobias, was drowned; the cut marks resulted from being cast about in the ditch; and the wound on the penis of the boy might have been caused by a thorn.[16]

The mood was somber at Engel's house. After his return from the castle, Engel talked things over with Brünnlein and Süsslein. His mother and wife were crying. Süsslein asked Moses of Bamberg what was happening to them. After some discussion, Engel and Süsslein hid their gold and silver. Engel paced up and down, his teeth chattering as if he had fever. Supper was ready; Süsslein brought Engel some food at the table but he only ate a little. Engel asked the others to eat, but nobody touched the dinner. In the words of Isaac, the family cook, all were "pale under the eyes."[17] Süsslein was again on the verge of tears. Moses told her it was all right to cry in times of need. She burst out: "Oh woe to me, they will take away my sons and baptize them. If only I did not have sons I would feel no pain." Moses tried to comfort her: "You shouldn't cry so hard. Maybe things are not going to be as bad as you think."[18] His words rang hollow, for in his heart he thought nothing good would come of the discovery of the dead child: "People would break their limbs and pay them for their work."[19] While Süsslein worried about her sons, Engel pondered what would happen to his wealth. According to Moses of Bamberg, Engel wanted to flee but could not bear to leave his possessions behind.[20]

Engel went over to join Samuel and Tobias. At Samuel's house, the mood was eerily calm. Old Moses, worn down by age and infirmity, had retired to bed before the commotion began. Schönlein and Mayer went to bed after supper. The couple did not talk about the dead boy; to Schönlein, her husband seemed neither sad nor troubled.[21] The others were in the cellar examining the dead boy.

The authorities arrived at Samuel's house between eight and nine in the evening—the podestà, Giovanni de Salis; the captain, Jakob von Sporo; and their men, bearing torches. The podestà ordered his servant, Ulrich, a big man, to carry the body to St. Peter's Hospital. The Jews present—Samuel, Israel, Tobias, Engel, Isaac son of Moses of Bamberg, Joaff, and Seligman the cook—were placed under arrest.[22] They were questioned by the podestà and shown the corpse. In spite of their protestation that the child had drowned accidentally, the podestà believed them to be guilty because, in the words of the trial record, "people who are killed bleed openly in the presence of evil men or murderers."[23] After hours of questioning, the Jews were conducted to the dungeon at the Buonconsiglio.

The arrests shattered any illusions of hope. At Samuel's house, Mayer and Schönlein awoke to the commotion. After the men were led away, many in the household began to cry. Exhausted, they tried to snatch a few hours of sleep. Schönlein, Brünnlein, and Israel shared one bed in the antechamber of the main room; Anna, who was sick, slept on the smaller bed. They woke up early Monday morning, promised one another to withstand all the tortures and pain of the world and not confess to any murder charge. Israel comforted his mother, reminding her that Samuel had many friends in the city; he would seek help. Moreover, his father would never confess to a crime he had not committed. Convinced that the Schweizer was behind this, Israel asked everyone to denounce the common enemy; Samuel would soon be freed.[24]

Once her husband, Engel, was arrested, Süsslein recovered her courage. She wrote a letter in German, addressed to the Jews of the Venetian town of Rovereto, half a day's journey to the south of Trent, informing them of the arrests.[25] Well-organized and connected, the Jewish communities of the "Most Serene Republic" would play the main role in the rescue effort.

With Tobias gone, Israel the painter decided to leave Trent immediately. During the early morning hours on Monday, 27 March, he passed by Engel's house, where Lazarus told him not to worry and tried to dissuade him from fleeing. Israel was unmoved but he did agree to take letters for Süsslein to Arck. He had not gone very far before he, too, was arrested.[26]

After the first batch of arrests, the podestà, Giovanni de Salis, resumed his investigations on that Monday morning. He ordered a notary to draw up formal charges against the Jews. Then, accompanied by two physicians and a lawyer, the podestà went to the Church of St. Peter. Simon's father, Andreas Unferdorben, was summoned; he identified his son and demanded vengeance against the Jews. The two physicians, Archangelo de Balduini and Giovanni Mattia Tiberino, examined the wounds on the body.[27] Master Archangelo testified it was his belief that the boy died late on Thursday (Passover). First he, then Tiberino, gave expert testimony: the soft limbs and unobstructed throat of the body indicated to them that the boy did not drown but had died probably on Friday and had been lying in the water for two days.[28] Turning to Andreas, the podestà again questioned his activities on Friday. Andreas and his friend Cyprian, who had persuaded the podestà to search Samuel's house on Friday, had actually tried to spy on the premises themselves.[29] The podestà was ready to take further action. He ordered more arrests: Israel son of Samuel, Old Moses, Mayer, Salomon (Tobias' cook), Lazarus of Saravall, Moses of Bamberg, Moses the tutor, Isaac (servant of Engel), Vital, and Brünnlein, Samuel's wife. In short, he arrested Brünnlein as well as all adult males of the Jewish community, except for Israel the painter, who was on the run. The other women were placed under house arrest in Samuel's and Engel's dwellings.

It was a busy day for the podestà, who took many depositions. First to testify was the night watchman, Antoniolio, who heard the crying of a child in Samuel's house Friday night. The man heard singing, then a child crying, followed by the words "*sweig pueb* " in German and "*täsi, täsi*" in Italian to quiet the boy. He had thought it was one of the Jewish boys.[30]

The investigators then went to inspect Samuel's house. The ditch that led into the water cellar was open to the streets; Simon's body could have flowed down the ditch from the neighboring house. Its owner, Neser Leder, told the podestà he had never seen the boy before.[31]

Returning to the castle, the podestà heard three accounts that convinced him that the Jews were guilty. Giovanni da Feltre, a convert, was imprisoned in the Buonconsiglio. Asked whether it was true that Jews needed Christian blood for ritual practices, Giovanni, baptized seven years before, reluctantly repeated a tale that Schachet, his father, who used to live in Landshut, Bavaria, had told him fifteen years earlier. In 1440, fifty-five Jews were burned in Bavaria for killing a Christian child, but Schachet had managed to escape. Asked whether his own father had ever used Christian blood, Giovanni was at first reluctant to answer. Eventually he said that his father used to put blood into a cup of wine before Passover, sprinkle it on the table before the evening meal, and curse the Christian faith. Blood was used in preparing matzos, although Giovanni claimed he did not understand the meaning of its use.[32]

The next to come forward was a German woman, Margaritha, nicknamed "the blond Gretchen" (*Gelbgreth ein teutsche zu Trennt*), who spoke no Italian. Frederico, a notary, was appointed interpreter. She swore an oath on the Bible and began her story. Fourteen years earlier, in 1461, her son Joachim, not quite three years old, had also been missing on Good Friday. She searched everywhere but could not find him. Urged by others, she approached Bishop Georg Hack (Hinderbach's predecessor) and asked him to search Samuel's house. Nothing was found, but she noticed a secret place in Samuel's shed. On Saturday she returned alone. She cried out her son's name and heard him answer "Mamma!" Blond Gretchen then went to fetch the priest; together they returned to Samuel's shed, where, under a pile of wood, they found little Joachim alive and well. Although the boy seemed unhurt, he died two months later. At the time, Blond Gretchen continued, Samuel denied any knowledge and said the boy could have slipped into the shed. In concluding her statement, Blond Gretchen said she did not recognize any of Samuel's current servants; she only recognized Brünnlein and their son, Israel, who had been a small child at the time of Joachim's disappearance.[33]

The last to testify was another woman named Margaritha, the wife of Hans Lederer. Asked whether she knew anything about the killing of Andreas' boy, she answered she heard nothing suspicious. Yet she did recall that on Good Friday, at about the third hour, when she was standing on the street talking to Trobar's wife, whose house was opposite Samuel's, she heard a boy crying but did not know where the voice was coming from. Then she said to Trobar's wife: "It seems to me it is the voice of Andreas' boy." After that she went home. Upon further questioning, Margaritha insisted she recognized Simon's distinct sobbing, different from other children's. That seemed to have clinched the case for the podestà and confirmed the Jews' guilt.[34]

In appearance, the podestà undertook the initial investigations according to due process. An *inquisitio* into a murder case was begun by the authorities, who questioned both medical experts and credible witnesses. Fundamental to the due process of inquisitio, however, was the assumption that the magistrates had every right to investigate persons of ill repute (*mala fama*) and that the testimonies were given by credible Christian witnesses. The Jews, by definition, were people of bad repute.

In reality, anti-Jewish prejudices superceded whatever caution a judicial process might have called for at this early stage. Among the authorities, both the podestà, Giovanni de Salis, and the physician Tiberino were natives of Brescia, where Bernardino da Feltre had preached against Jewish usury. Da Feltre's anti-Semitic Lenten lectures had created an atmosphere in Trent receptive to accusations of blood libel against the Jews. Among the neighbors, the rumor of child murder readily became a suspicion, if not a certainty, once the body was found. Overnight the Jews, familiar and somewhat intimate neighbors, were transformed into strange murderers, and old prejudices seemed confirmed by yet another "Jewish crime." Giovanni de Salis was ready to begin the interrogations.

CHAPTER FOUR

THE TORTURE CHAMBER

Towering over the city of Trent, the Castello del Buonconsiglio, a formidable fortress built between 1239 and 1255, was modified several times during the fourteenth and fifteenth centuries, when it became the residence of the prince-bishops. Although windows and openings were added to the inner court and the façade facing the city, the castle still retained the character of a massive stronghold, constructed out of wood and ashlar. Built into the city wall, the Buonconsiglio consisted of three levels, divided into rooms and chambers for various functions, including separate areas for the prince-bishop, the captain, and the podestà. A round tower, rising above the fortress complex, anchored the city's defenses. Within its stone walls were prison cells and the torture chamber.

Considered essential to criminal investigations, the application of judicial torture in early modern Europe followed established procedures, which were supposed to prevent the abuse of suspects by overzealous officials. The communal statutes of fifteenth-century Trent specified that when a suspect was to be tortured by the podestà, two citizen councillors, called *Gastaldioni,* had to be present during the interrogation, to intervene, if necessary, when the podestà applied excessive torture.[1] The standard mechanism of torture was the *strappada,* for which the victim had his hands tied behind his back with a long rope and was then hoisted up in the air by a pulley. Left dangling several feet from the ground, the victim would thus face the judge, who was attended by the scribe recording the interlocution and the prison guard doubling as torturer. Judicial procedure allowed for the gradual escalation of torture. If the victim refused to confess, the torturer would abruptly let loose the rope (*cavalete*), a practice frequently repeated; in the YM the scribe also referred to this as "letting the prisoner jump." If that method failed to produce the desired effect, other painful refinements were inflicted, such as whipping with the rope (*squassatio*) or adding weights to the feet of the dangling victim.

Already persuaded of the actuality of ritual murder, the magistrates in Trent devised a strategy to extract confessions by first interrogating the subordinates of Samuel's household; only after cracking the accomplices would they go after the main culprits, the three Jewish householders.

Israel's cousin, "the Other Seligman," was the first to appear before the magistrates, on 27 March.[2] Barely twenty years old, Seligman was terrified by the sight of the torture chamber. After some preliminary questioning, as the recording clerk tells us, "the podestà, seeing that he did not want to reveal the truth, ordered him to be stripped, bound, and hoisted up."[3] His hands tied by a tight knot, Seligman panicked and said he would tell "the truth." To save himself, Seligman made up a story that revealed the tension within the small Jewish community. He told the magistrates that Engel's servant, Isaac, had told him he had killed the boy; that the Schweizer brought Simon to Engel's house alive and received twenty guldens for his efforts, that Isaac struck the boy in the neck so Simon coughed up blood, and that the Schweizer carried the boy into Samuel's house.[4] Naming the Schweizer was of course expected; he had a feud with the Jews and might well have initiated the accusation. But in ascribing the leading role to Engel's household, albeit in an attempt at self-preservation, Seligman revealed the tensions within the community between the two established families and the newcomer.

Next to be interrogated was Seligman the cook, who had discovered the body of Simon. On 28 March, Seligman was led into the torture chamber. Facing him were the podestà, the captain, the Gastaldion Antonio Geruasi, Odoric von Breggen, Hans von Calapin, and others.[5] Asked whether any Christian had visited Samuel on Good Friday, Seligman answered that Claus Metzger and his wife came to redeem a pledge.[6] Impatient with the preliminary questioning, the captain ordered him to be stripped, bound, and hoisted up.[7] Seligman was asked to tell the truth. After dangling for some time, he was let down by the magistrates, given a seat, and asked to repeat the conversation in Samuel's house after the discovery of the body. The magistrates also asked Seligman why the foreign Jews did not flee, to which the reply was that they thought "the evil" would not befall them.[8] In all, this session was rather inconclusive; the magistrates had applied moderate force but Seligman did not confess. Nevertheless, they had enough to go on and were determined to step up the torture.

The next day, 29 March, the tower guard, Hans, brought two more prisoners before the magistrates. Vital, Samuel's servant, immediately accused the Schweizer of killing Simon and pinning it on the Jews.[9] After the Schweizer had lost his lawsuit disputing his wife's wages for attending Samuel's daughter-in-law's labor, he had often threatened Samuel, according to Vital. But the magistrates did not want to hear this tale; they wanted "the truth" and put Vital to the strappada. Later in the day, they questioned Israel, Samuel's son, who maintained his ignorance of the reasons for his arrest. He, too, was tortured.[10]

Next, the magistrates dealt with their chief suspects, the Jewish householders. On Friday 31 March, they questioned Samuel and Engel. Led into the captain's room from his cell in the Buonconsiglio, Samuel, knowing full well the reasons for his arrest, calmly recounted the discovery of Simon's body in his cellar.[11] Making no progress with this line of questioning, the magistrates ordered Samuel removed to the torture chamber, where the interrogation resumed. The subject of ritual murder came up immediately; the scribe wrote down this interlocution:[12]

> QUESTION: Did he [Samuel] during his lifetime ever hear that a lost child is captured or killed by Jews?
> SAMUEL: No. Only once, during the Lenten period when Hermann lost a child. He was asked to help look for the child but refused. Later, the boy was found.

At this point, the record tells us, Samuel was ordered hoisted up.

> QUESTION: Did anyone come to him on Holy Thursday or Good Friday?
> SAMUEL: A peasant, whose name he cannot remember. He believes no Jew had murdered the child; it must have drowned.
> QUESTION: Who is the priest among them?
> SAMUEL: There is none.
> QUESTION: Who dispenses the sacraments and sings?
> SAMUEL: There is no distinction in rank during the service.

This line of questioning revealed the thinking of the magistrates. The "truth" of the crime was accepted; what they needed to establish was the motive for such an inhuman act, whose explanation had to lie in the dark secrets of the Jewish religion.

The magistrates persisted in the same line of attack when interrogating Joaff.[13] As he had fished the body out of the water, the podestà asked him how the child got there in the first place. Dangling from the rope, Joaff insisted that the Jews were framed: "It is not true that Jews kill Christian children. He has only heard this charge from Christians." After a while, unable to withstand the pain, Joaff said he would tell the truth. Trapped in the horrific logic of the torture chamber, he did not know what story was expected of him; the magistrates interpreted his equivocation to be a sign of his guilt and kept applying force. The clerk recorded for posterity the absurdity of the word game:

QUESTION: When was he in the synagogue?
JOAFF: He said he could not remember and did not know anything about the boy's death.
QUESTION: Why does he speak about the child's death, when nobody has asked him anything?

The same day, the magistrates questioned Engel twice, but he revealed nothing under torture.[14]

The magistrates also questioned Christian witnesses. On 31 March, the magistrates interrogated the Schweizer, whom they had arrested three days earlier after Seligman had denounced him as the child-killer; his wife, Dorothea, was likewise brought in for questioning.[15] A laborer, the Schweizer farmed land leased from a lord Jakob, a canon of the cathedral.[16] Sharecropping was typical in the Trentino, a region rich with vineyards and a major exporter of wine to the Tirol.[17]

Questioned without judicial torture, the Schweizer recounted his whereabouts between Thursday and Saturday during Holy Week. He told of toiling in the fields on the hillsides outside the city walls; he mentioned meals taken with friends at home, with Cyprian, Bertold, and others; he repeated what he heard about the missing boy, and how some had suggested he had drowned while others said the authorities should look in Samuel's house. His testimony painted a picture of his neighborhood, a crowded and yet public space with ditches, contiguous houses, common walls, with windows, holes, and openings. He recounted visiting many churches, to hear mass and to receive indulgences. He described searching for the boy well into the night, together with his friend Cyprian, piercing the darkness of the ditches with torches. He told the podestà the worried parents consulted a wise-woman (*vaticinatrice*) to find the missing boy. Throughout his testimony, the Schweizer did not hide his dislike for the Jews. He acknowledged a dispute with Engel over wages owed his wife, but added that the matter had been resolved. For Christians who associated with the Jews, the Schweizer had nothing but scorn. He accused Roper the tailor of telling his Jewish friends everything that went on with the Christians. He suggested to the podestà that Old Johannes the gravedigger, who had worked for the Jews, could have carried the boy into Samuel's house.

The Schweizer had a ready alibi. On Holy Thursday, the day of the purported murder, he claimed to have worked all day in the vineyards. Dorothea corroborated his alibi, informing the magistrates that she took food to her husband in the fields. Satisfied with their testimonies, the magistrates did not inflict judicial torture. This single occasion on which they interrogated the Schweizer was conducted according to due process, although they did not release him until April.[18]

The prejudice of the podestà is clearly revealed by his different treatment of the Schweizer and Roper. Whereas Giovanni de Salis did not consider the Schweizer a likely perpetrator and released him after one session without torture, he suspected Roper of being an accomplice to the Jews and questioned him under torture. Roper was arrested on 31 March and interrogated on April 2 and 7, the second time with the aid of the strappada.[19] Roper recounted his whereabouts on the days in question and stuck to his answer under torture. His friend Wolf Holzknecht corroborated the testimony.[20] The podestà released Roper on 18 April. Understandably, during the interrogations Roper played down his association with the Jews. But as we have seen, he was a friend of Samuel and his family. In a later interrogation, Old Moses remembered that, a few days before Passover, a tailor swore he would never gamble again after losing twenty ducats at a card game in Samuel's house. Old Moses did not know the name of the tailor but it was likely to have been Roper.[21] In spite of his incarceration and torture, Roper remained a steadfast friend to the Jewish families.

The breaking point came during the first week of April. After adjourning on Sunday, the magistrates renewed their work on Monday 3 April, determined to escalate the measures of torture. For the prisoners, hardly recovered from their previous interrogations, it meant a new round of ordeals. The podestà renewed his questioning of Samuel, Engel, and Vital; Tobias, Old Moses, and Mayer were put to the rope for the first time.

Vital broke down after two torture sessions; he confessed to "the truth" but was unable to come up with the specific details the magistrates wanted to hear.[22] The podestà then proceeded with full force against the three Jewish householders.

Samuel withstood the torture without confessing. On the strappada, he said he knew "the blond Gretchen" but denied she had ever accused him of kidnapping her son. Stating he had never done anything wrong, Samuel told the magistrates they were doing him an injustice. Left dangling in the air, he asked the podestà where he had read or learnt that Christian blood was useful in Jewish rites. Giovanni de Salis answered he learnt it from the Jews and asked for "the truth, the truth!" The scribe recorded the following scene:

> He [Samuel] answered: He has said it and they are torturing him unjustly. At that, it was ordered to make him jump two or three arm's length. So there he hung and said: "God the Helper and Truth help me!" And after he had been hanging for two-thirds of an hour, it was ordered to let him down and return him to prison.[23]

Samuel's interrogation resumed on Friday 7 April. The magistrates meant business. Tied to the strappada, left dangling for fifteen minutes, wood tied to his legs, repeatedly given jolts of the rope, and having sulfur in a frying pan put under his nose, Samuel was at the end of human endurance. Wishing no doubt to spare as many lives as possible, Samuel confessed that only he and Tobias had choked the child to death with a handkerchief. The magistrates were not satisfied; they wanted to know about the wounds. In bitter irony, perhaps, Samuel said: "I have told the truth."[24]

Engel confessed the next day. After being interrogated and tortured on 3 and 7 April, Engel appeared yet again in the torture chamber on Saturday 8 April. His will broken by repeated torment, Engel described the "crime" for the magistrates. The three householders had conspired to get a Christian child for its blood; Tobias actually kidnapped Simon; Engel saw the dead child on the almemor but did not know how it died. As for the motive of the alleged ritual murder, Engel explained that Jews used blood to celebrate Passover when the Red Sea turned into blood and destroyed the Egyptian army.[25] Satisfied they had finally penetrated the hidden meaning of Jewish rituals, the magistrates released Engel to rest his bruised limbs in his dark cell.

Hitherto spared the torturer's rope, Tobias came in for the fury of the magistrates. The author-editor of the Yeshiva manuscript identifies him as "the traitor, seller, and handler of the innocent blood of Simon the martyr of Trent."[26] Every passion play required its traitor; every Christ-like martyr demanded his Judas. Tobias, the physician who cured Christians in Trent, played the ascribed role with pathos.

His first interrogation, on 3 April, seemed to go well. Facing the magistrates in the captain's room, Tobias described the discovery of the body, the conversations among the Jews, and the decision to report the find to the authorities. As a trained physician, Tobias also volunteered his opinion on the cause of death and the wounds on the corpse. The magistrates adjourned for supper. After the meal, they summoned Tobias to the torture chamber. Hung in the air for half an hour, with the torturer "striking with the rope repeatedly," Tobias stuck to his answer. The magistrates sent him back to the cell.[27]

On 7 April, Tobias was again questioned. He was asked whether he had ever heard that Jews kill Christian children; Tobias replied that he had heard it only from some Christians and that the charge was not true. The magistrates questioned his whereabouts on Holy Thursday (the day of the alleged murder). Impatient with his answer, the podestà ordered Tobias pulled all the way up; from that height the jolt could very well have dislocated his shoulders.

Tobias cried out he would tell the truth and begged to be let down. "He was let down," the scribe tells us, "and it looked like he was completely senseless or ruined. When he began to come to his senses, the podestà asked him to speak the truth."[28] Since Tobias could hardly speak, Giovanni de Salis adjourned the questioning until the next day.

Tobias returned on Saturday a completely broken man. Convinced they had at last cracked open the heart of the case, the magistrates worked Tobias over on Saturday and Sunday to obtain a full description of the alleged ritual killing.[29] Over these two days, 8 and 9 April, Tobias spun this tale of murder, duly recorded and perhaps elaborated by the scribe: on the eve of Passover, Samuel suggested they should get a child; the task fell upon Tobias. He enticed Simon with sweet words to come with him and handed the sacrificial victim over to Samuel. On the day of Passover, Old Moses covered the boy's mouth while the others stuck the child with pins and tore out his flesh; his blood was collected and distributed. Later, the dead child was thrown into the water by Samuel and Isaac. Tobias was not present at the killing, only rabbis possessed the knowledge of the rituals. In the minds of the prosecuting magistrates, Tobias's confession established the scenario of the "real crime." All subsequent interrogations would follow this basic script as the magistrates tortured more corroborating details out of the other prisoners. The imagined torture of Simon seemed to justify, nay demand, the judicial torture of the Jews. With details embellished by the moral indignation of the Christians, this fantastic tale would become in time the history of the Trent ritual murder.

Even the eighty-year-old Moses did not escape torture, although the magistrates summoned the physician, Master Archangelo von Capeis, to be present during the questioning. When asked why he was arrested, Old Moses kept quiet for a moment and said: "God would never help him again, if he and the other Jews were not innocent of the child's death." Old Moses continued, in the words of the scribe, "It is forbidden in the Ten Commandments to kill and Moses [the Prophet] also forbade Jews to eat blood; when they slaughter an animal, they first drain its blood." Hoping to persuade the magistrates by history, Old Moses told them that thirty-five years earlier, in 1440, in Meran (a neighboring town to the north of Trent populated by German speakers), an enemy of the Jews "planted" a dead child in a Jew's house, accused him before the captain, who almost put the Jew to torture. The Jew, however, hid nothing; and the captain arrested the Christian who confessed to the frame-up. Unmoved by this moral tale, the magistrates put Old Moses to the rope.[30] Three days later, 7 April, the magistrates strung up Old Moses's son, Mayer, in the same room; in spite of repeated torture, Mayer refused to confess.[31]

After Samuel's confession on 7 April, the magistrates put Israel, his son, to torture for the second time. On 9 April, they tortured Israel into accusing his own father of offering a hundred ducats for a Christian child. To save himself from further agony, Israel invented a long narrative of the tortures of Simon and the eventual disposal of the body.[32]

Worked up to a frenzy by the multiple confessions of murder, with contradictory details of motive, torture, and cover-up, the authorities were determined to get to the bottom of what seemed an endless spiral of violence. To achieve their ends, the magistrates cranked up the machinery of judicial violence. Between 10 and 16 April, they conducted a total of eighteen sessions (surpassing the previous week's tally of fifteen), putting eleven of the fifteen imprisoned men to the strappada. Three aspects of the behavior of the magistrates stand out: first, they granted no respite between interrogations, stepping up instead the intensity and length of torture; second, they persisted in asking details of the Seder, trying to reconstruct every detail of Simon's painful death, extracting every shade of meaning of blood symbolism, and recording with great care every Hebrew word associated with the imagined killing rite; finally, they encouraged the Jews to incriminate one another in order to escape further torture.

Some of the Jews held out, repeating their innocence over the screams of torment and stern questions; others broke down, blaming themselves and others in this grotesque elaboration of the fictive murder ritual. Still others retracted their confessions during moments of lucidity and respite from the rope, only to be tortured more severely into retracting their retractions. A few wanted to confess but could not anticipate the murder script written in the minds of the magistrates and, thus, continued to suffer; a handful, who desperately held onto reality, tried to incriminate themselves while excusing their loved ones and subordinates from the charge, willing victims in a coercive sacrifice that demanded live offerings.

Six men had been interrogated at this point. The magistrates now set out to break their last resistance and to extract confessions fully consistent with the scenario of the murder described by Tobias. On 10 April, they broke both Seligmans. After suffering repeated tortures, inflicted by men who crossed the boundary from the legally sanctioned to the sadistic, Seligman the cook confessed: he described the Seder service, during which Old Moses, Tobias, and Samuel stuck the boy with needles and tore off his flesh with pincers, satisfying the enraged magistrates with this tale of bloodthirsty Jews.[33] "The Other Seligman," under torture, incriminated his kin, Samuel, in the killing of Simon.[34] The magistrates, however, wanted details. The next day, they tortured Seligman, asked leading questions, and coerced him into telling a tale that turned the synagogue into a chamber of horrors, where, on Good Friday, the Jews inflicted various tortures on Simon. The smallest details of his account agreed with the confessions of Seligman the cook still fresh in the magistrates' minds. The scribe carefully transliterated the Hebrew words from the Haggadah that supposedly accompanied the imagined ritual torturing of the Christian child, who "breathed his last," in the words of the trial record, "died crosswise at the hour of Christ's crucifixion and hanged its head to the side."[35] Were these the words of Seligman, the magistrate, or the clerk? It is impossible to distinguish among the voices. It was as if the imagined world of the torturer and the victim had become one.

Harsh taskmasters in the name of justice, the judges permitted themselves, perhaps, a sense of satisfaction: the stubborn Jews, schooled by the instruments of torture, had at last understood the meaning of the trial; they now spoke the language of Christian martyrdom, however imperfectly, for they were, after all, not native speakers. Most important, they were translating for their Christian judges—to their horror and fascination—the hidden meaning of Jewish rites, an evil sign, a murderous discourse, a counter-language to the liturgy of Christian piety. Even the stubborn Engel now seemed to understand. Tortured again on 10 April, Engel confessed. In the Yeshiva manuscript, the author-editor noted in red ink (as distinct from the black ink of the protocol) Engel's admission of guilt: "Thereafter he confesses correctly."[36] Engel repeated the Hebrew prayers, told of the slow, painful death of Simon, the collection of blood, and the disposal of the body. Questioned about the meaning of the wounds on Simon's body, Engel said they corresponded to Moses' curses on the Egyptians, an answer apparently deeply satisfying to the magistrates, for they stopped the torture at this point. Resigned to his own fate, Engel still tried to defend his housefolk, telling the magistrates that neither his wife nor his household knew of the ritual killing.

Tobias also tried to save the women. Questioned for the fifth time on 17 April about who was present during Passover, he said the women were absent from the killing because they did not participate in the service.[37] Determined to fathom the secrets of Jewish rituals, the magistrates questioned Tobias closely about the meaning of various gestures and Hebrew words, especially the Haggadah curses against the Egyptians, all duly recorded by Hans von Fondo, the clerk. If Simon was killed during Passover that year, the magistrates reasoned, how many other innocent Christian children had already perished at the hands of the murderous Jews? One purported murder triggered imaginings of multiple slaughters. A single criminal investigation evolved into a Christian representation of Jewish rituals and now constructed a history of blood killings in order to legitimize its own proceedings.

Like any good "ethnographers," the judges launched into a
research of the origins and the history of the phenomenon they
had just reconstructed from the testimonies of the tortured Jews:

> QUESTION: How long has he been the head of the household?
> TOBIAS: Maybe thirteen years.
> QUESTION: How did he manage all these years with Christian
> blood?
> TOBIAS: He had never needed Christian blood until the time
> when Samuel, Engel, Moses, and himself discussed and raised the
> issue.

Angered by the answer, the podestà ordered Tobias to be led to
the torture chamber. Tobias cried out: "For God's sake, don't! I
will tell the truth."[38]

To satisfy his tormentors, to escape further suffering, Tobias
elaborated his tale: Yes, four or five years ago, he had paid one
gulden to a pious Jew, Abraham, for Christian blood. Insatiable for
details, the podestà pressured the storyteller to make the tale
more "real." Tobias thus described Abraham, a man he might have
actually known, as between "thirty-five and forty years old, pale
under the eyes, with a medium size beard, wearing a gray cloak
and black hat." The magistrates wanted more. Tobias continued,
"Some six or seven years ago," adding more exotic details, "when
the Emperor was visiting Venice, he was there too. A Jew from
Candia, a great merchant in the imperial entourage, sold sugar
and blood. This man, with a long full beard and a great coat, was
between forty-five and fifty, but his name was unknown."[39]
Pleased with the stories, the podestà questioned Tobias a little
more, without torture, and concluded the interrogation. The
questioning had satisfied the need for narrative details; it produced a "realistic story," with characters, actions, and motives.
Later that day, the count of Terlaco, one of the jurors present
during the session, read back the confession to Tobias, in German
translated from the Latin notes.[40] Tobias agreed to this version,
for he hardly remembered the many tales he told. In his case the

storyteller had no claim to his material; only the audience did. This was, in any case, his final performance.

Those who had already been tortured eventually learned to play the roles assigned to them by the magistrates. On 12 April, Vital was led to the torture chamber for the fourth time but withstood repeated hoistings.[41] The next day, the magistrates asked Vital leading questions based on Tobias' confessions. Vital broke down. He told of "the killing." But when the captain asked him to testify against Israel, "he did not answer and looked at the captain with blank eyes."[42] The result of his lack of cooperation: torture. On 14 April, more torture.[43] On 15 April, the fourth straight day of the rope, Vital confessed to torturing Simon.[44] As a reward, the judges allowed him three days to recover before putting him to the ropes again on 18 and 21 April.[45] With every jump, every scream, Vital learned a few lines of the script: yes, the stabbing, the needles, Christian blood for matzo, the insults to the boy, Simon's body on the almemor, and other details already well rehearsed by other Jews.

Mayer grasped more quickly the logic of the torture chamber. Dangling on the rope on 11 April, he recounted the torture of Simon, in conformity with the official story, and answered the many queries on Christian blood: they shed Christian blood to scorn Christ and to prepare matzo and added another invented "history" of a blood transaction, four years earlier, from a Jacob of Saxony.[46] On 17 April, Mayer heard the accusation and his own confession read back to him in German; he signaled consent, in effect, to his death warrant.[47]

The more the Jews were tortured, the more ghastly was their description of the ritual murder. The prisoners seemed to transform their own pain into a creative energy, both to avoid being tortured and to satisfy the violent demands of their Christian tormenters that they inflict fictive harm on a dead child. In the interrogation of 11 April, for example, Mayer, after confessing to witnessing the ritual murder, explained to the magistrates that it was done out of scorn for Christ.[48] Vital, tortured for four consecutive days, collapsed, confessed to torturing the boy himself. Delirious with pain during two more torture sessions on 18 and 21 April, he described the prolonged agony of Simon's Passover torments.[49] The imagined torture of the synagogue and the real suffering of the torture chamber joined, and the logic of pain created its own discourse and validation. Vital confirmed for the magistrates every detail of Tobias's confession, while incriminating the physician as the most bloodthirsty murderer.

Not everything went smoothly. In the frenzy of interrogations, the torture machinery occasionally broke down, as it did during the further interrogations of Israel, Samuel's son. On Thursday 13 April, the magistrates questioned Israel on the Passover meaning of Christian blood:[50]

> QUESTION: Why the blood?
> ISRAEL: If they don't use blood they'll stink.
> QUESTION: Why do they drink and eat blood?
> ISRAEL: After the custom of painting blood on the post in Pharoah's times.
> QUESTION: What words were used when they killed the child?
> ISRAEL (in Italian; the interlocution had been in German): Cosy fato al dio cristiani chi non e vero dio e che veginca zentilomini suli cavalli e sula gabelli.[51]

The logic of torture was reinforced by the promise of yet more torture; it was pointless to admit guilt. Israel now denied everything he had previously confessed. At this point, the author-scribe of the Yeshiva manuscript, reflecting the feelings of the officials at the trial, added this comment (again marked off by red ink from the black ink of the main text): "Note here how often he [Israel] changes his words and contradicts all aforementioned things, thus one has to interrogate him from the beginning."[52] Fierce in its power to elicit mimicry, the logic of torture could only teach the subjugated to parrot the sound of the master language, not to grasp its grammatical structure—the discourse of ritual murder was impossible for Israel to learn. The next day, the magistrates repeated their lesson: they tortured Israel, asked for the truth, and heard the reply, dutifully copied down by the clerk: "He had said it and whether he hangs there thirty or forty years, he has nothing else to say."[53] Israel's defiance and endurance lasted precisely one more day; he confessed to the details of the supposed ritual murder on 15 April.[54]

Then there were those who had not begun this harsh playacting. Bit by bit, day by day, the magistrates had already extracted confessions from Samuel, Engel, Tobias, Israel, Mayer, Old Moses, Joaff, Vital, and the two Seligmans. Interrogated for the first time the third week of April, another five men—Lazarus, Israel the painter, Moses of Bamberg, Moses the tutor, and Isaac—had no idea of their ascribed roles in the ritual murder drama. Tortured repeatedly on 12 and 13 April, asked to tell the truth, Lazarus, Engel's servant, replied to the judges: "Tell me what I should say and I will say it."[55] The authorities, likewise, got nothing useful out of the others: Isaac said nothing incriminating;[56] Moses of Bamberg told the magistrates his life story and said, when put to the rope, "Just make it quick so I can die fast."[57] Moses the tutor, also known as "Young Moses," and Israel the painter both emphatically denied that Jews committed ritual murders. During the interrogation of 12 April, the law clerk Hans von Fundo recorded these words of Young Moses:[58]

QUESTION: Since the body was found in Samuel's house, someone in that household must have done it, is it not?
MOSES: Jews did not kill the boy; it is against their commandments.
QUESTION: Could one of Samuel's servants have killed the boy?
MOSES: He does not know. He believes the boy had drowned.

Even more directly, Israel told the magistrates, on the same day: "Although the Germans say Jews kill Christian children, it is not true."[59]

The torture chamber served the magistrates well: almost all the Jews had broken down and confessed. The stage was set for sentencing. But the executions of the Jews, the triumphant demonstration of Christian piety, would have to wait. On 21 April, Jacob von Sporo, captain of Trent, informed his colleague Giovanni di Salis that the trial had been suspended. The order came from Innsbruck, issued by Archduke Sigismund of Tirol, who had a Jewish physician in attendance and to whom the captain owed allegiance. As the representative of Johannes Hinderbach, the podestà had to acquiesce, for Hinderbach had pledged allegiance to Sigismund. Confronted by this unexpected turn of events, the prince-bishop emerged from the shadows to become the vigorous defender of the *causa Simonis*.

CHAPTER FIVE

"BLESSED SIMON MARTYR"

J ohannes Hinderbach wrote a letter on May 1 to Raffaele Zovenzoni, poet laureate of Trieste, inviting him to compose verses in honor of the "blessed martyr Simon," so that the people would know of his miracles. Expressing his regret that just punishment could not yet be meted out to the Jews, Hinderbach complained of the various machinations devised by the Jews to turn Archduke Sigismund against the trial.[1] Against the intervention of a secular prince, only Christian piety could prevail. "Blessed Boy, lament bitterly to the Emperor and Duke," wrote Zovenzoni in his hymn to Little Simon. A native of Istria, who spent some years in Venice as a client and friend of patrician humanists, Zovenzoni became Hinderbach's ally in promoting Simon's cult in Venice.[2] For Hinderbach and his entourage, the propagation of Simon's martyrdom was central to his defense of a "fair" trial. Who would be a more devastating accuser of the Jews, who could testify more eloquently to the zeal of the bishop and the righteousness of his actions, if not the little boy martyr? And who else could be his most devoted follower in death, if not the prince-bishop, his temporal and spiritual lord in life?

The first miracle was reported on 31 March and became the first entry in the "Book of Miracles of the Blessed Simon Martyr of Trent."[3] Between 31 March 1475 and 29 June 1476, no fewer than 129 miracles were attributed to Simon.[4] Pilgrims came to Trent, prayed, and donated money. Some were healed; all left carrying word of the wondrous event. From the start, Hinderbach took a personal interest in the pilgrimages, recording in his almost illegible German and Latin the sums collected from the pious visitors and the monies paid out for various expenses associated with the cult.[5]

By letters, by word of mouth, by travelers' tales, and by sermons, knowledge of Simon's martyrdom in Trent spread rapidly in the Veneto, Lombardy, and Tirol, often inciting mob violence against the Jews. The doge of Venice, Pietro Mocengio, expressed his concern for the safety of the Venetian Jews in two letters, addressed to the podestà and captain of Padua (22 April 1475) and to the captain in Friaul (28 April 1475).[6] It had come to his attention, Mocengio informed his officials, that on account of the rumor that the Jews of Trent had murdered a child, Christians had been attacking and robbing traveling Jews in Venetian territory, so that the Jews feared to undertake any trips. The ringleaders of the violence were certain preachers. The doge did not believe the rumor. Therefore, not only should the officials protect the persons and property of the Jews, they were to prevent the preachers from inciting the populace to anti-Semitic violence.

If preachers conjured up Christ, saints, and martyrs when fueling popular violence against the Jews, the poets invoked the Muses, Apollo, and Virgil "in praise of him, Blessed Boy Simon, slaughtered by the Jews."[7] The most elegant Latin of the humanists expressed the vilest hatred of Jews; and the sweet Virgilian meters framed violent messages of expulsion from Christian lands. Thus Zovenzoni began his hymn by invoking the pope, emperor, dukes, prelates, and magistrates to expel the Jews; he ended the poem with an apostrophe (not forgetting to praise Hinderbach), admonishing Emperor Friedrich and Archduke Sigismund to avenge with flames "the crime" of the Jews.[8]

Hinderbach, who fancied himself a humanist, also tried his hand at Latin verse. Although his poetic talents proved unequal to Zovenzoni, his sentiments echoed the hatred of the poet laureate, castigating the Jews as blood drinkers and blasphemers. He called upon all Christians to expel them from their communities.[9]

Poetic truth persuades only believers; the power of authenticity to convince belongs rather to prose. The most inflammatory rhetoric came from the pen of Giovanni Mattia Tiberino, one of the medical doctors who examined the corpse of the boy on Easter Sunday. Personal physician and friend of the prince-bishop, thoroughly informed of the interrogations, Tiberino was utterly convinced of the guilt of the Jews and tirelessly propagated the "martyrdom." On 15 April, in the midst of the interrogations, he composed a long letter, in elegant classical Latin, addressed to the Senate and people of Brescia, his *patria*:

> I write to you, magnificent rectors and most famous citizens, of a great thing which occurred a few days ago, which has never been heard of before, since the passion of Our Lord to our own age, which Jesus Christ Our Lord, as much out of pity for the human species as the horrible crime that has to be stomached, has nonetheless brought forth to light, in order that our Catholic faith, if it is weak in part, may create a tower of fortitude, and that the ancient infestation of the Jews may be wiped out from the Christian orbit and the living memory of them may completely disappear from the earth.[10]

Not only did the Jews oppress Christians by usury, Tiberino continued, they sucked the blood out of Christian children in their synagogue and inflicted sufferings on the boy Simon, just as they did to Christ.

With poetic license, Tiberino constructed the "dialogue" in the house of Samuel that led to the abduction of Simon "one thousand four hundred seventy and five years since the Incarnation of the Word." To mock Christ, the living Word of God, the Jews had to represent their evil in unspeakable words and ritual; to expose their crime, the Christian had recourse to that language of moral suasion, humanist Latin. Thus Tiberino had the Jews lament that they lacked but one thing for Passover: "Then, throwing their eyes around one by one, without a word, all knew they were talking about sacrificing a Christian child, whom they would slay atrociously in contempt of our lord Jesus Christ." After much deliberation and disagreement, on account of the anticipated danger (Tiberino cleverly utilized the contradictory statements extracted under torture to create a narrative plot), the Jews urged Tobias to procure the child, since he had daily contacts with the Christians thanks to his medical practice. At first Tobias refused, but threatened with the ban and lured by the promise of wealth, he agreed, claiming he had too many sons to feed—Tiberino was careful here to create narrative twists and depict motives, in order to endow his story with the aura of authenticity.

The letter continued with a long description of the abduction. When Tobias presented the child to the Jews in Samuel's house, they yelled excitedly in anticipation of tasting Christian blood. Tiberino chose the onomatopoeic "*ululare*" to describe the imagined yelling, to mark off the barbaric Jews from civilized Christians, for barbarity consisted not only in bloodthirstiness but also in the very sound of human speech. "Ululare" was the battle cry of the Germanic tribes, as described by Tacitus, whose own ancient Roman tongue became the model of civilized expression in the Renaissance humanist revival of classical culture.

Turning to the scene of the search, Tiberino adopted the rhetorical trope of the Gospels: "Meanwhile, the mother of the boy, Maria, when she saw that he was absent, not only searched for him among neighbors, as she was accustomed to do, but, with a stricken heart (*percusso pectore*), together with her husband,

Andreas, explored the entire city." In Tiberino's humanist Latin, Simon's mother assumed the persona of the *Mater Dolorosa,* whose heart was pierced by sorrow for the death of her son, Jesus Christ.[11] Tiberino did not leave it to the reader to draw the parallel. In the next sentence, he described the Holy Spirit's inspiring the search for the boy among the Jews, who "suspended him crosswise (*in cruce*) in contempt of the Christian faith."

Little Simon's death was represented in the epic mode, in Virgilian meters. Describing the time of sacrifice, Tiberino borrowed verses from the *Aeneid:* "It was the time when the human heart was refreshed by the first quiet and when human and canine voices grew quiet."[12] The physician, perhaps to be expected, described the imagined killing in vivid detail, the particulars of which have been repeated in numerous later representations. The Jews were described as "atrocious," Simon's blood as "sacred," and his death as representative of the passion of Christ. In Tiberino's words, "and extending violently both of his sacred arms, in the manner of the crucifix, others, raising their weapons, sank them hard in the reclining sacred body; then, all gathered around, saying: *tolle Yesse Mina, elle parachies elle pasissen tegmalen,* that is, just as Jesus God of the Christians, who is nothing, we butcher this one, and thus confound our enemies in eternity." In the description of the moment of death, Tiberino resorted first to the language of the Vulgate Bible—"and lowering his head he gave up his holy spirit to the Lord"—and, again, to Virgil.[13]

Tiberino went on to describe the effort to conceal the corpse, its display on the Sabbath in the synagogue, its disposal and discovery in the ditch, the actions of the podestà and captain, and the miracles. And he continued, "Behold, Christian faithful, Jesus crucified between thieves. Behold the Jews did this so as to have power over Christians. Glorious Simon, virgin martyr and innocent, hardly weaned, and whose speech has not reached human eloquence, was extended crosswise by the Jews in contempt of our faith." After alleging a litany of blasphemies from the Talmud, Tiberino informed his reader that "the most glorious Simon" was born on 6 December to very poor parents, Maria and Andreas, and that on account of this, all the Jews, old and young, had been incarcerated and would receive their just punishment.

The pamphlet became the most influential piece of anti-Semitic propaganda surrounding the Trent ritual murder trial, not only because Tiberino was a physician , but because his letter to Brescia, an impressive display of rhetoric, constructed a story of pathos and verisimilitude. Entitled *Passio beati Simonis pueri Tridentini*, the first edition was published in April 1475 by Bartolomeo Guldinbeck in Rome, who brought out two more editions by July of the same year, and another in 1476. In addition to the four Roman editions, ten other Latin editions appeared in print by early 1476: two each in Treviso and Venice, one each in Vicenza, Mantua, Nuremberg, Cologne, Augsburg, and Trent. In September 1475, a German translation was published in Trent by Albrecht Kunne of Dudestadt, the first printed book in the city. Two more German editions appeared, in Augsburg in 1475 and in Nuremberg in 1476.[14] A Latin poem by Tiberino, "I am the boy Simon," also circulated widely in Italy and southern Germany; it was reprinted as late as 1511 in Augsburg.[15] A German poem, composed by Matthäus Kunig, was published in Venice.[16]

Thus the printing press, introduced to Italy from central Europe, with many German masters among the first generation of printers, was indispensable in creating a major cultural event out of the Trent blood libel. Far from reflecting a mood of optimism, often attributed to the revival of classical learning, this new technology expressed the deeply felt anxiety of Christian Europe. Threatened by heretics and Jews from within, Christendom was also besieged from without by the Turks. Among the four books known to have been published by Albrecht Kunne in Trent were two works on Simon and two on the Turks, including one published in 1475 on the fall of the Crimean city of Caffà to the Ottomans.[17]

In Tiberino's treatise on the "Passion of Simon," we find most of the iconography of later representations. Three central themes established the identification between Little Simon and Jesus. The first was their common "passion," dominated by the motif of the crucifixion. The other two motifs, reflecting popular Renaissance Christian piety, concerned the wounds on Simon's genitals and the portrait of his family.

The official story of ritual murder gave considerable attention to Simon's genitals. On the judicial level, the attention might simply have resulted from the medical examination, which noted cut wounds on the penis. But seen in the context of Renaissance iconography, aside from the fundamental fear of castration, the cutting of the genitals, understood as a distorted representation

Figure 3. Simon of Trent. From the *Nuremberg Chronicle* of Hartmann Schedel (1493). Note the prominence of circumcision as an iconographic motif, in contrast to Baroque representations (fig. 10). Reproduced courtesy of the Beinecke Rare Book and Manuscript Library, Yale University.

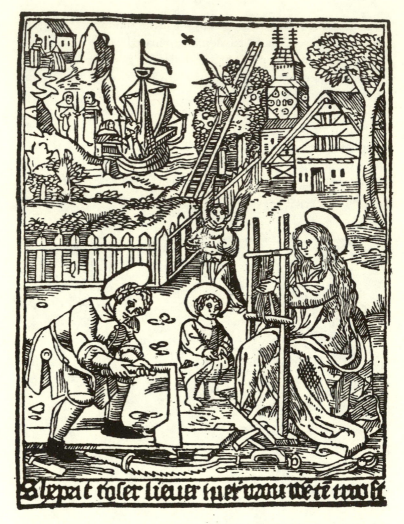

Figure 4. Two representations of the Holy Family. Woodcuts,
late fifteenth century.

of circumcision, revealed the distinction between Christians and Jews. The ritual that marked Jewish males included, of course, the child Jesus; if Simon's death was to be an imitation of Christ, he, too, would have to undergo circumcision.

The iconography of Simon's death explicitly and prominently represented the wounding of his genitals, as in the woodcut that accompanied the 1493 Nuremberg *Weltchronik* of Hartmann Schedel, prepared by the workshop where Albrecht Dürer was an apprentice. The woodcut shows a boyish penis, small, not erect, a sign of childish innocence. The wounds on Simon's genitals implied both the violation of innocence and the redemptive nature of human flesh and blood. In Renaissance art, the uncovered penis, a central motif in depictions of the Infant Jesus and the crucified Christ, revealed the humanity of the Christian savior. Human sinners were saved, not by some abstract promise of redemption, but by the torment of a real man, the Son of God, whose genitals indicated his participation in and transcendence of sensual human nature.[18]

Little Simon, remembered as a child of poor parents, also reflected the enormously popular late medieval Christian devotion to the Holy Family. According to the trial record, Engel's servant Lazarus told the magistrates that Samuel had compared Simon to Jesus, both being born out of wedlock.[19] Whether Samuel actually made the comparison matters little, compared to the evocative power of the portrait of Simon and his parents as a poor, innocent Christian working family, cruelly persecuted by the Jews. The Holy Family was similarly represented in late fifteenth-century woodcuts as familiar neighbors and a model household. A woodcut from 1460, for example, depicted a toddler Jesus riding his hobbyhorse, with Saint Dorothea looking on; another woodcut from the same period showed an older boy Jesus helping Saint Agnes with a wine press; while a third, from around 1490, represented Joseph, Mary, and Jesus as an ordinary hardworking family.[20] Indeed, the notion that the otherwise unremarkable little Simon came from a family of common folks fitted perfectly with the ideals of humility, innocence, and sacrifice, the emotive forces in the Christian drama of salvation.

CHAPTER SIX

THEATER OF DEATH

J akob von Sporo informed his colleague, Giovanni de Salis, on 5 June that permission had arrived from Innsbruck to resume the trial against some Jews but not others. Together, the captain and the podestà would finish up the legal proceedings against the Jewish householders, including Engel, who was under the jurisdiction of the castellan, the nobleman Hans Regner, and also Old Moses, Vital, Israel, and "the Other Seligman;" they could not, however, proceed against the women and the other household servants.[1]

The next day, they moved against Samuel, who had hitherto refused to confess to a detailed ritual murder scenario. As the leader of the Jewish community, to whom the leading role in the alleged ritual murder was ascribed, his confession was essential. After several sessions with the rope, Samuel told the magistrates he would tell the truth. On the verge of triumph, the magistrates demonstrated their magnanimity by sending their prisoner back to his cell in order to recover his memory and strength.[2]

On 7 June, Samuel was again in the torture chamber, but he kept silent. The rope, once more. So futile, this expression of courage: did the magistrates have some respect for his endurance? In any event, it was simply a matter of time. The clerk recorded the following scene:[3]

> PODESTÀ: He should no longer keep silent because his accomplices have told the truth.
> SAMUEL: Even if they said something they still had not told the truth.
>
> Now someone told the podestà, if you give some holy water, "*weichpruen, acqua benedicta,*" to malefactors to drink, they would confess to the truth. Thus the lord podestà gave Samuel a spoonful of aforementioned water to drink. . . . After it was given and Samuel had drank it, he was asked to tell the truth. He responded he did. And then two hot eggs were then placed under each of his armpits. When they were thus placed he was asked to tell the truth.
>
> SAMUEL: He will tell the truth to the captain and the podestà.

The captain and the podestà cleared the torture chamber. Later, they informed Hans von Fundo that Samuel had promised to tell the truth if they promised death by fire and not any other kind of death, which the notary duly recorded. The other witnesses were called in; Samuel was set down from the rope; and the party moved to the captain's chamber to hear Samuel.

The notary set down Samuel's confession: On the eve of Passover, Tobias, Engel, and Samuel met in the synagogue to discuss getting a Christian child. They asked two German Jews—Lazarus and David, guests staying with Samuel and Tobias—to procure the child. When this scheme did not work out, Tobias volunteered. Beloved by the people for his medical practice, Tobias would arouse the least suspicion. He was the ideal man. Samuel promised to do all he could for Tobias for as long as the physician stayed in Trent. The following day, Tobias came back with a child under his cloak; Samuel fed the child honey and food.

After copying down this testimony, the notary continued with a long description of the alleged torture of Simon as confessed to by Samuel, on which the author-editor of the Yeshiva manuscript commented, in red ink: "Let one note also the meaning of the contempt and dishonor against Christ, and the curses and vengeful prayers against the Christians."[4] To intensify the emotional power of this story and to bolster its authenticity, the magistrates asked Samuel to repeat in Hebrew the Haggadah curses against the Egyptians, which were immediately transliterated and translated into Latin, and later written down, in an unsteady Hebrew script, in the trial manuscript.[5]

Hans von Fundo the scribe then noted, with reference to Samuel's confession, the disposal of the body and the time spent in tearing out Simon's flesh (half an hour). As material evidence, the magistrates showed Samuel a bench from the synagogue on which Old Moses supposedly held the boy and cut his penis. Samuel acknowledged that he recognized the bench.[6]

Samuel continued his confession: Italian Jews had been practicing ritual killing for a long time; a child under seven would be murdered to imitate the crucifixion of Christ for "Christianity threatened to outshine and eclipse Judaism." Moreover, Jews used Christian blood for matzo. All these things, Samuel continued in his grotesque confession, he had learnt from Rabbi David Sprintz in Bamberg and Nuremberg some thirty years before.[7]

Interested in other possible murders, the magistrates asked Samuel for details: in 1473, when the Eysenposch child was missing and then found, Bishop Hinderbach had ordered the child to be examined for cut marks. The suspicion of ritual murder, as the trial record reveals, long predated the accusation of 1475 and originated from none other than the prince-bishop.[8] More details were narrated to satisfy the magistrates. Four years before, according to the notary's transcript of Samuel's words, he and

Tobias purchased Christian blood from a traveling Jew, a man from Saxony, who had a recommendation from Rabbi Moses of Hall.[9]

Facing his torturers and judges, longing for deliverance and a quick death, Samuel plumbed the depth of his memory. Summoned from events long past, acquaintances ancient and recent, seen in the eyes of the mind, now paraded before his accusors as fellow accomplices in the murder of Christian children: his teacher, Rabbi David Sprintz, and a nameless traveling Jew from Saxony who once sought his hospitality. The torture controlled not only Samuel's body; its logic also extorted from his memory narrative fragments for the story of ritual murder. Deprived of his past, at least in public remembrance, Samuel could only hold on to his life story in private memory, a realm violently shut off from posterity, except for distorted glimpses from the official story.

It was a remarkable confession. How did Samuel come up with the corroborating details? What happened in the torture chamber, when the magistrates dismissed the witnesses and the clerk? The detailed story of Simon's death, the official story, was already in circulation as early as the beginning of April, when Tiberino wrote to Brescia. Did the magistrates repeat to Samuel the scenario of the imagined murder they had constructed from the other confessions? It seemed likely, since they opened the interrogation by telling Samuel the other Jews had confessed. Why did Samuel confess? First of all, he must have realized the futility of resistance; the magistrates were determined to obtain a confession. Moreover, a quick resolution to the trial, he might have thought, would still save the women and children, and possibly some of the other imprisoned Jews as well. Thus, death by fire, a martyr's death, represented the only honorable escape. Unfortunately, like the scribe and witnesses, we are also shut out of the torture chamber when the podestà cleared the room and can only imagine the conversation between Samuel, the podestà, and the captain.

The magistrates were not done with their storyteller. On 11 June, they summoned Samuel, not to the torture chamber but to the captain's chamber, where the prisoner embellished his story on the disposal of the body and uses of Simon's blood. A central motif emerged: the blood had to come from a Christian martyr, otherwise it was useless for the Jews.[10] The text clearly points to a different narrative direction, moving away from the actions of the Jews to the representation of Simon's martyrdom.

Although Samuel was the main target of the magistrates after the resumption of trial, they conducted other interrogations. On 9 June, they put Vital to the rope. In April the poor man had confessed to the alleged murder but seemed confused about the details. Now, after Samuel's confession and more torture, Vital in the words of the clerk, "told the truth as it is, and in the same way as the others."[11]

On 10 June, Israel, Samuel's son, confessed to a premeditated cover-up, to which his kin had agreed.[12] Thus, the magistrates explained, to their immense satisfaction, the stubborn refusal of father and son to confess for so long—one more proof of the logic of the torture chamber.

Old Moses was the first to fall victim to the "Evil" that plagued his people. Tortured only once initially, on 4 April, Old Moses had been languishing in his cell for more than two months when he appeared on 9 June before the magistrates. Eighty years old, his health broken by incarceration, Moses "looked dumb (blöd) in anticipation of pain," as the clerk observed. Giovanni de Salis strung him up a bit, put two hot eggs under his armpits, and then sent the old man back to his cell.[13] The following day, 10 June, the podestà threatened Old Moses with the rope; and the old man talked. He confessed to the "conspiracy" to kidnap Simon, to Tobias' role, to the prolonged tortures, to his own guilt, to the imitation of the crucifixion, and to the martyr's blood; in short, he confessed to the official story of ritual murder. Then, Moses undertook a journey through his past, in search of episodes, in order to answer the query about other blood transactions.[14]

Another detail fascinated the magistrates: the imaginary wounds inflicted on Simon. On 11 June, they interrogated "the Other Seligman," who said, while hanging from the rope, that Old Moses cut the boy's penis, while the others held the boy crosswise to imitate the crucifixion of Christ.[15]

Eighty-one days and sixty-four interrogations after the initial arrests, the magistrates set a formal court date of 14 June to announce charges. One by one, Samuel, Old Moses, Vital, and "the Other Seligman" were brought from their cells to the captain's chamber. When Samuel entered the chamber, he faced the podestà sitting on the judge's bench. Others were present: Parteline of Capesar, a Venetian doctor of civil law; five men fluent in both German and Italian who served as interpreters—Count Anthon von Terlaco, Dr. Hans Anthoni von Vaschet, Dr. Odorich von Brixen, the notary Peter Rauter, and Odorich of Bergamo; also present, among others, were Augustin von Brigno, Julian Gardel, Hans Tysenreuth, Hans Pheiler, and Schare von Bozen.

Before announcing the charges, Giovanni de Salis explained from the judge's bench:

> He knew and understood that the aforementioned Samuel was a German who knew both German and Italian well . . . however, to facilitate explanations and understanding, he ordered the notary, that Count von Terlaco . . . would translate into German, all that is contained in the written Latin statements, which the notary would duly record, also that he [Terlaco] would translate back into Latin for the podestà and notary, faithfully and in good conscience, all that the aforementioned Samuel might answer in German.[16]

The podestà then read the court statement "as he had taken and formulated from the written confessions of aforementioned Samuel Jew, in accordance with law and custom."[17] After the reading of the long Latin statement, describing the charges against Samuel and his confessions, Terlaco first translated the charge into Italian, then into German for Samuel. At the end, Samuel swore an oath in Hebrew, attesting to the veracity of his confession. Giovanni de Salis gave Samuel three days to think of possible defenses. Through Terlaco, the podestà asked Samuel whether he wanted an advocate and assigned von Vatschet as his attorney.[18]

The charge against Samuel was blasphemy against the Christian faith; in murdering the child, Samuel was doing "devil's work."[19] Following the recitation of formal charges, the podestà sentenced Samuel to be carried to the execution site on a wagon, his flesh to be torn out by glowing pincers, and to be burned at the stake.

On the same day, Vital, Old Moses, and "the Other Seligman" also heard their charges through interpreters.[20] The podestà sentenced all three to death at the wheel and stake. Old Moses escaped the humiliation of a public execution. The guard found him dead in his cell; "He took his own life, as one said," was the laconic comment of the scribe.[21]

The first batch of executions took place between 21 and 23 June: nine men—Tobias, Engel, Samuel, Israel, Old Moses, Mayer, Vital, and the two Seligmans—had been sentenced to death, but Moses had already taken his own life. The first prisoners executed were Samuel, Israel, Engel, and Tobias. Presiding over the executions were the notary Peter Rauter and Christopher of Venice, both citizens and Gastaldiani; Hans von Farin assisted in supervising the ritual of death.[22] Transported on a wagon, bound for the execution grounds outside the city's St. Martin's Gate, where bloodshed would not pollute the civic community, the Jews played their final role in this theater of death. As ordered by the podestà, Samuel had his flesh torn out by pincers en route, a torment reserved for the gravest offenders condemned under the criminal code. The citizen-councillors, however, took pity on the prisoners and did not bind the Jews to wheels to have their limbs broken. Tied to the stake, with flames leaping around them, did they utter silent prayers, or did they implore the Lord aloud to fortify their faith? For the Christian multitude, however, the message was clear: the executions represented both a redemptive drama and a theater of horror. The murderous Jews, so the officials proclaimed, had inflicted unspeakable tortures on a little Christian boy; they suffered now their own indescribable agony at the hands of triumphant Christian justice. As the flames consumed flesh and blood, as the ashes hovered in the air, the spectators felt deeply the power of both the Christian faith and its official guardians.

Four more executions were scheduled for the following day. At the last minute, the two Seligmans asked for baptism; the captain immediately postponed their executions. Vital and Mayer's sentences were promptly carried out—death by burning at the stake.[23] On 23 June, both Seligmans were baptized, then beheaded and burned post mortem.[24] For the Trentini, the conversions only confirmed the guilt of the Jews and reflected the wonders of their little martyr.

CHAPTER SEVEN

THE APOSTOLIC COMMISSIONER

In the early summer months of 1475, Bishop Hinderbach vigorously promoted the cult of Simon. To correspondents in Venice, Vicenza, Innsbruck, and Rome he sent letters, distributed Tiberino's treatise and little images of Simon's martyrdom. Mobilizing a network of humanists, preachers, jurists, and courtiers, Hinderbach hoped to defeat the spokesmen of the Jewish communities, who were pleading their cause with the emperor, the archduke, and the pope.[1] They accused Hinderbach of undertaking the trial only to lay his hands on Jewish money; moreover, the Trent Jews had been severely, unlawfully tortured and summarily executed.

In a letter dated 23 July, Pope Sixtus IV admonished the prince-bishop to wait for the arrival of the papal envoy and suspend the trial "because many and important men began to murmur" about the conduct of the Trentini.[2] In the instructions to the commissioner, Baptista Dei Giudici, dated 3 August, the

Holy See authorized Dei Giudici to prepare an authentic copy of the trial records, secured with the seals of the bishop of Trent and the commissioner, to be forwarded to Rome. The commissioner was also charged to investigate the facts of the trial, particularly regarding the truth of the alleged ritual murder and the nature of the many miracles attributed to Simon. Empowered to repossess any properties of the Jews that had been illegally confiscated, Dei Giudici was charged with freeing the still imprisoned men, women, and children. He was to transfer the investigation to another place, should conditions in Trent prevent the execution of the mandate. And finally, the pope urged Dei Giudici to exercise the utmost prudence and seek the cooperation of the bishop of Trent.[3]

Born in Finale in the Liguria, Baptista Dei Giudici was forty-six or forty-seven years old when appointed apostolic commissioner by the pope. Son of a noble family, Dei Giudici entered the Order of Preachers at a young age. He spent the better part of his adult life in Bologna, a member of the Dominican community and student of theology at the university. Active in promoting reform within the Dominican order, Dei Giudici was appointed bishop of Ventimiglia in 1471 by Pope Paul II. When the Franciscan Francesco della Rovere was elected Pope Sixtus IV, Dei Giudici, a compatriot from Liguria, found favor in Rome, becoming, thanks to his reputation for piety and learning, a member of the Curia, the fulcrum of Christian power.[4] Dei Giudici was appointed commissioner both on account of his upright character and also, in his own words, because "he often preached and wrote against the Jews and had never, in all his life, even once shared a meal or a drink with any Jew."[5] By selecting Dei Giudici, Sixtus IV wanted to preserve papal impartiality, balancing the petition of the Roman Jews for an apostolic commission with the appointment of a man whose anti-Judaic sermons would seem to preclude any objections from Trent.

Hinderbach, however, from the beginning suspected the commission of sympathizing with the prisoners. Traveling to Trent via Ferrara, Vincenza, and Padua—not the most direct route—Dei Giudici took almost a month to reach Trent, a complaint that Hinderbach subsequently raised, accusing the commissioner of contacting the Jewish communities en route.[6] On 2 September, Dei Giudici arrived in Trent and stayed twenty-two days. What we know of the commission comes from the two bishops— Hinderbach and Dei Giudici—after their open confrontation and the transfer of the investigation to Rome.[7] From the acerbic ad hominem accusations hurled by the two principals in their appeals to the commission of cardinals, we can reconstruct the events surrounding the apostolic commission in Trent and the bitter controversy it provoked.

The beginning, at least, was auspicious. When the entourage of the apostolic commission reached Trent, they found a throng waiting at the gate in their honor, with Bishop Hinderbach at its head, leading both lay and ecclesiastic members of his court, the greater part of the cathedral canons, councillors of the commune, and a host of citizens.[8] Dei Giudici entered the city in procession and was escorted to a house near the Buonconsiglio, where he received many distinguished visitors, including envoys from Archduke Sigismund, who were themselves investigating the trial in Trent.[9]

In spite of private doubts—Hinderbach suspecting the commissioner as pro-Jewish, and Dei Giudici questioning the conduct of the entire affair—the two parties maintained formal cooperation until the departure of the commissioner. Anxious to promote Little Simon's "martyrdom," Hinderbach arranged for Dei Giudici to visit St. Peter's to view the corpse, which had not been moved from the church since Easter Sunday in March, when the body was discovered. Many men and women were eager to testify to the miracles effected in Simon's name. On 6 September, a few days after the viewing, the commissioner wrote to Cardinal Stefano Nardini:

Yesterday I went to see the body of the boy together with the reverend Lord Bishop and many other citizens and canons. When the bishop curiously inspected and moved the shin bone, such a stench emitted [from the body] that I had an attack of cholic, not quite strong enough that I was to vomit, but enough that I could have vomited at any time. However, I could not do such a thing, for indeed everyone and many who know me well saw that my colors were changing. The bishop himself, seeing that I was agitated, asked me whether it was on account of the stench. I responded yes and said we should leave for I was unable to suffer any longer. He then said the same had happened to him at first but now he was accustomed to it. Then I said: "Reverend Lord, I am surprised that your Lordship would display the disclosed body this way, for it is horrible to behold and it would be better if it is put in a coffin." He said that he had a little embalming casket made, but the people did not want the body removed.[10]

Unimpressed by the small decomposing corpse, Dei Giudici had his assistants question three or four witnesses to extraordinary events attributed to Simon; he found that the alleged miracles "were described in a mendacious, fraudulent, and deceitful manner."[11] Instead of hearing about miracles, the commissioner insisted on examining the original trial records. Hinderbach objected: this, being a temporal matter, was beyond the jurisdiction of the commissioner. The trial records must not be made public, lest the Jews took advantage of the knowledge; Dei Giudici should concentrate on Simon's martyrdom. Eventually Hinderbach relented, as the request clearly accorded with papal instructions. Permission was given to the podestà, who read the proceedings aloud to the commissioner. After more negotiations, Dei Giudici was allowed to prepare a copy, which his notary, the priest Raphael, duly made. Even then, Sigismund's envoys accused Raphael of altering the text and making another secret copy for the Jews, a suspicion perhaps first suggested by the Trentini. Dei Giudici offered to appoint another notary—a man by the name of Arnald Plak, who was fluent in Latin, Italian, and German—but the Trentini refused. Their motive, according to Dei Giudici, "was to create suspicion of the councillors and assistants of the commissioner, so that afterwards, they could defame and refuse the same commissioner."[12]

On another matter, Hinderbach absolutely refused to cooperate. In spite of repeated requests to talk to the incarcerated Jews, either in front of the prince-bishop or other citizens, Dei Giudici never saw the prisoners. In his subsequent polemical letter, Hinderbach admitted his reason: from the beginning he was suspicious of "the lord commissioner who sought with every effort to liberate [the Jews]. . . It was to be feared that if he talked to them, he or his men could give some sign to the Jews, who would be rendered more obstinate, since they were always saying, 'A man will come to free us.'"[13] The commissioner did succeed in talking to the painter Israel, who had accepted baptism in April and was later released and lived under his Christian name, Wolfgang (see chapter 9). Through him, Dei Giudici heard a first hand account of the torture and passed on messages to the Jewish women, who were under house arrest.

Dei Giudici fell sick. Later, back in Rome, he would attribute the cause to his lodgings in Trent and Hinderbach's inhospitality:[14]

> But that same Bishop of Trent prepared the worst and most dishonorable hospice near his castle, in which he [the Bishop of Ventimiglia writing in the third person] spent twenty-two days in great discomfort and at his own expenses, often ill on account of the bad room which was very wet and which, since its ceilings were exposed, was often rained on, to the extent that it was sometimes necessary to spend several nights out of bed, since the room was flooded with rain. There were even puddles of water, excrement, and filth; nobody could go to him and reveal secrets, nor could he exercise his own tasks. Such was the surveillance of the men of the bishop of Trent.

Staying in a commune seized by passion for its new martyr, dealing with authorities who were hardly cooperative, the commissioner decided it was dangerous to prolong his stay. There were death threats. Apparently, Dei Giudici openly expressed doubts about the miracles, and "many people, moved more by furor than reason, temerity than devotion, threatened to kill the commissioner in the streets of the city, if he did not confirm the miracles and the asserted martyrdom." For several nights, Dei Giudici had an armed guard posted at his door. If it was indeed Hinderbach's strategy, as Dei Giudici later charged, he succeeded brilliantly: getting the commissioner to examine the miracles not only distracted him from the trial records, but also stirred up the populace against the skeptic.[15] For his part, as Dei Giudici recalled later, "he imitated the apostle Paul, who freed himself by his astuteness from the clutches of the Pharisees," men who pretended to piety, "with words and actions worthy of vipers."[16]

When his notary finished copying the trial record, Dei Giudici departed for Verona, citing his bad health. He left Trent on 23 September. In public, both parties still maintained the façade of cordiality. Hinderbach provided a cart for the journey and sent two officials, with their servants, to accompany the commissioner. Disturbed by the presence of Jews in Dei Giudici's entourage, Hinderbach sent along officials in order to obtain reliable reports on the commissioner's activities. But two could play the game. When the episcopal deputation returned to Trent, the Jews bribed Hinderbach's servant, named Christian, to smuggle letters to the imprisoned women.[17] In this case, Christian was discovered and imprisoned overnight in the tower, but the commissioner and the Jews succeeded in getting word to the women in Trent. Finally, the party reached Rovereto, half a day's journey (about seventeen miles) to the south, three hours after dark. The next day, still preserving the peace, Dei Giudici wrote to Hinderbach, to inform him of the journey.[18]

Within the territory of the Venetian Republic, Rovereto, although a small commune, lay beyond the jurisdiction of the bishop of Trent. Later, Dei Giudici would recall the reason for the departure: in Trent, his life was threatened and witnesses dared not speak their minds; in Rovereto, he was "under the protection of the most illustrious lordship of the doge of Venice, where justice was and would always be dispensed, where innocent people are not killed, where Christians do not plunder Jews, as it was in Trent."[19]

For the moment, Dei Giudici did not want an open confrontation. In his letter of 24 September, Dei Giudici informed Hinderbach of a meeting with Jewish representatives in Rovereto. Among the spokesmen of the Jewish communities, several described themselves as advocates for the Jews. They implored the commissioner not to move on to Verona but to attend to their cause and secure justice in Rovereto. When the Jewish advocates went to Trent, they were afraid to ask for safe-conducts due to mob violence: innkeepers refused them lodging, and many threatened to kill them and their servants if they dared to defend the prisoners. Furthermore, the advocates asked Dei Giudici for a copy of the trial record. Their intention was not "to defend the dead, who cannot rise again, but the truth; and they wanted to defend the cause of the living, both the incarcerated, but also those in all the world, who would be in danger, if the trial record is held to be true because it is said to contain the confessions of all the Jews, that from decade to decade, especially in the year of the Jubilee, they use the blood of Christian boys."[20] A skillful diplomat, Dei Giudici implored Hinderbach to see what a labyrinth he was in and assured the prince-bishop, in a postscript, that the trial record would not be opened until it reached Rome.

Having used the pretext of this meeting, Dei Giudici directly yet courteously presented his request. In a letter dated 26 September, written in a friendly manner, the commissioner asked Hinderbach to release the innocent Jews in accordance with the papal mandate. He closed his letter to Hinderbach, still in a humble tone (perhaps with irony), with news of his improving health.[21]

With the cooperation of the Rovereto authorities, Dei Giudici was conducting his own investigation into the alleged child murder in Trent. The key witness for the apostolic commissioner was a resident of Trent, Anzelino Austoch. On 28 September, the podestà of Rovereto issued a safe-conduct order for Anzelino to travel into Venetian territory.[22]

Since the apostolic commissioner had turned to the Venetians, the prince-bishop sought support among the Germans. On 29 September, Hinderbach composed an open letter, in German, in his own defense, addressed to the princes of the Holy Roman Empire.[23] Knowing full well that Trent was by no means the first ritual murder trial, Hinderbach appointed an envoy, the Dominican Heinrich of Schlettstett, to gather testimonies of previous trials in southern Germany. The friar arrived in Ravensburg on 3 October. With the cooperation of the local authorities, a document was properly drawn up, signed, and sealed. Written by Johannes Truchsess von Waldburg, imperial bailiff of Lower and Upper Swabia, the notarial instrument testified to a trial against the Jews of Ravensburg in 1430 on account of a purported child murder in the cellar of one of their houses and the subsequent executions of the accused Jews. Attesting to the sworn testimony were three imperial notaries, Johannes Ungemut, Franz Spuoll, and Johannes Branndis, all of Constance.[24]

The next stop was Pfullendorf. There, Friar Heinrich got five witnesses among the magistrates to testify to an alleged ritual murder committed in 1461 by the local Jews. After taking the sworn testimonies of Johannes Dalat, Johannes Dankingen, Johannes Pluin, Peter Pastlin of Andelspach, and Johannes Sutor, the two notaries—Peter Spät of Ehingen, imperial notary in Constance and protonotary in Pfullendorf and Johannes Bustettee, imperial notary in the diocese of Constance—attached their seals and signatures.[25] Traveling further north in the Upper Rhine valley, on 21 October, the friar arrived in Endingen, still within the diocese of Constance but politically in Habsburg territory, not far from Freiburg, where, as recently as 1470, a notorious ritual murder trial had destroyed the local Jewish community.[26] Having completed his mission, the Dominican returned to Trent, where the newly acquired documents were added to the legal arsenal of Bishop Hinderbach.

While the good friar was on his way, the apostolic commissioner broadened the attack; he brought to Hinderbach's attention the papal letter which prohibited any preaching on the subject of Little Simon's martyrdom.[27] On 5 October, Jacob of Rippa, one of the Jewish advocates, presented a list of charges against the highest officials in Trent, accusing the prince-bishop, the captain, and the podestà of instigating the ritual murder trial in order to despoil the Jews.[28] On 8 October, Dei Giudici excommunicated Giovanni de Salis, chastising the podestà of Trent for twice disobeying his mandates.[29] On 12 October, Hinderbach sent his secretary, Johannes Mensche, to Rovereto to protest Jacob's charges. The envoy also objected to the commissioner's judicial intervention but extended an invitation from Hinderbach, who promised Dei Giudici better accomodations if he would return to Trent, which would be a more suitable place to conclude the business of the Jews.[30] Dei Giudici sent a polite reply but essentially ignored the protest.[31] Six days later, the apostolic commissioner issued an injunction, ordering de Salis to appear in Rovereto and face the charges brought by Jacob of Rippa.[32]

In the meantime, Anzelino Austoch left Trent for Rovereto, apparently lured by the promise of money in exchange for his testimony, not knowing he was a prime suspect, and was promptly thrown into prison by the podestà of Rovereto, who was acting under the order of the apostolic commissioner.[33] Put under judicial torture, Anzelino accused the Schweizer of killing Simon and framing the Jews. From previous testimonies, the Schweizer was known as an enemy of Samuel. Was Anzelino his partner in crime? The Trentini were nervous. To undermine this testimony, Hinderbach had the Schweizer re-examined to counter the renewed suspicion. On 13 October, without the application of torture, Johannes Vogler, canon of the cathedral and acting vicar for the prince-bishop, questioned the Schweizer and released him after Dorothea, his wife, again testified to her husband's presence in the vineyards on the day of the alleged child murder.[34] In the battle of testimony and rumors, Hinderbach's partisans seemed particularly active. The story went around that Anzelino was tortured into implicating the Schweizer, that he subsequently retracted his confessions, and that Dei Giudici surrounded himself with Jews.[35]

In the larger campaign, however, the apostolic commissioner was gaining the upper hand, at least momentarily. During October, the barely cordial disagreement between Hinderbach and Dei Giudici broke out into open confrontation. To the prince-bishop, threatening signs appeared on the horizon. On 10 October, Sixtus IV wrote to the doge of Venice, admonishing him, on pain of excommunication, to protect the Jews and silence all sermons on Simon's martyrdom.[36] On 12 October, Sixtus IV wrote to Hinderbach, informing the prince-bishop that letters from Hinderbach himself, the apostolic commissioner, and Archduke Sigismund had arrived in Rome. On the question of the trial, the pope admonished Hinderbach to release from imprisonment the women and children, whose innocence was considered beyond doubt, especially since incarceration would aggravate the illness of the women.[37] On 24 October, Dei Giudici wrote to Hinderbach, informing him of the many Jews from Verona who had come to plead on behalf of the Jews in Trent.[38] In another letter, signed two days later and invoking papal authority, Dei Giudici asked Hinderbach to release the imprisoned Jews.[39] On 29 October, Dei Giudici sent letters to the prince-bishop, the podestà, the captain, and the city councillors of Trent, calling for the release of all of the prisoners—men, women, and children—and the transfer of the trial to Rome. Expressing regret that his previous edict was not followed, Dei Giudici admonished the Trentini not to torture the prisoners and to comply with his mandate within three days on penalty of excommunication.[40] These letters provoked a strong protest, dated 31 October, in which Bishop Hinderbach, the captain, and the podestà accused Dei Giudici of exceeding his commission and intervening in the affairs of secular authorities. It was surely not the intention of the pontiff to release the Jews before the trial was concluded, the Trentini argued. Moreover, suggesting that the commissioner was corrupted by the Jews in Rovereto, the protest accused him of failure to cooperate with the bishop of Trent in carrying out the mandate of the apostolic commission.[41]

In early November, Dei Giudici again admonished the Trentini to free the women and children, sending along a letter from Sixtus IV which prohibited sermons on the alleged martyrdom of Simon.[42] The Trentini raised objections, made trouble, and dragged their feet, but eventually released the Jewish children.[43] An impasse was reached. Based on his investigations, the apostolic commissioner had come to the conclusion that whatever the original motives, the trial against the Jews was conducted in the most inappropriate manner, with indiscriminate and excessive application of judicial torture. The confessions, extracted under torture, proved nothing. There was enough evidence, from the testimony of Anzelino, that the Schweizer might have killed the child and placed the body in Samuel's house. Worst of all, the bishop of Trent and his officials had refused to aid his commission but instead had abetted the popular superstitions surrounding the cult of Little Simon.

Hinderbach was outraged. Supporting the podestà and the captain, sticking to the official story of ritual murder, the prince-bishop resented the intrusion of the apostolic comissioner. After all, who was the bishop of Ventimiglia in comparison to a prince of the Empire? A fair trial against the Jews had been interrupted; suspicion had been cast on the conduct of Christian authorities; and the holy martyr, Little Simon, had been ridiculed. What could have motivated Dei Giudici, a man of the Church, to oppose such a pious and just undertaking? On 28 November, Hinderbach denounced Dei Giudici to the pope, accusing the apostolic commissioner of accepting Jewish bribes and of falsely imprisoning and torturing Anzelino in order to save the Jews.[44]

In mid-November, Dei Giudici left Rovereto for Verona, with a reluctant Anzelino in his entourage. During his stay in Verona, a plot was concocted to free Anzelino: armed men carried out the assault but were captured by troops sent by the magistrates, who had been instructed by the Venetian Senate to offer Dei Giudici "every assistance."[45] Dei Giudici arrived back in Rome on 1 December to lay down his charge. To repair the damage caused by the apostolic commission, Sixtus IV appointed a special congregation of six cardinals to examine the trial in Trent. While the cumbersome machinery of papal government bestirred itself, the authorities in Trent rushed to conclude their trial. Let us go back to October and follow the events in Trent after the departure of the apostolic commissioner.

CHAPTER EIGHT

AN ETHNOGRAPHY OF BLOOD

As summer turned into the golden days of October, with sunshine flooding the vineyards around Trent, the affair reached an impasse. Much was at stake. Christians and Jews, pope and emperor, commoner and magistrate, all had their attention on Trent. The attitude in Rome seemed ambivalent, reflecting in part, the usual opacity of the curia, and specifically, Sixtus' preoccupation with the Jubilee and Italian politics.[1] Hinderbach needed allies. In confronting the apostolic commissioner, Hinderbach emphasized his role as secular prince of a territory, owing allegiance only to the emperor. Before long, news from Innsbruck strengthened his hand.

Captain Jakob von Sporo received a letter on 20 October from Archduke Sigismund, authorizing him and the podestà to interrogate the remaining Jews. Sigismund wrote:

> We advise you, Our beloved faithful servant, that concerning the Jewish men and women you have in prison, that you render

justice as it should be, and let the death sentences be carried out, and whatever verdict is pronounced, you should comply, so that you would fulfill our Christian opinion. Issued in Meran on Friday after St. Gallen's [20 October], in the year of Our Lord, 1475. [To] Our faithful, beloved Jakob Spawr, Our Captain in Trent.[2]

The second phase of the ritual murder trial, from late October 1475 to mid-January 1476, involved six men—Joaff, Isaac, Lazarus, Moses of Bamberg, Moses the tutor, and Israel the

Figure 5. Sigismund of Tirol. Engraving from Domenicus Custos, *Die gefürsteten Grafen zu Tyrol,* 1599. Reproduced courtesy of Tiroler Landesmuseum Ferdinandeum, Innsbruck.

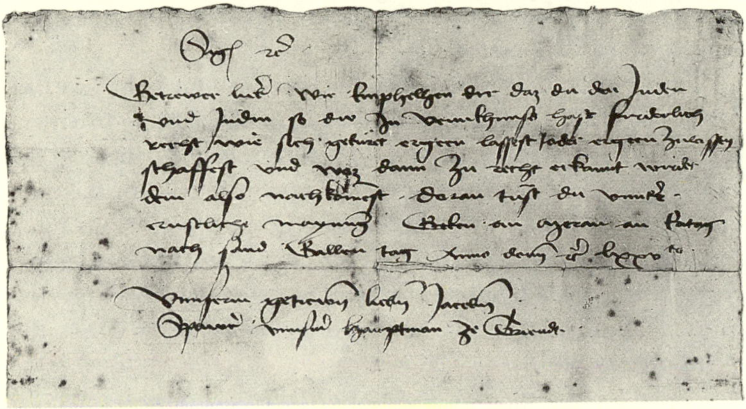

Figure 6. Letter from Sigismund of Tirol to Captain Jakob von Sporo, dated 20 October 1475. Reproduced courtesy of Archivio de Stato, Trent.

painter; during this period, several of the Jewish women were also examined, although intense interrogations did not proceed until the early months of 1476. With the exception of Israel, baptized Wolfgang in April, the authorities saw the men as accomplices in the crime, although they were outsiders and travelers. Israel's interrogation and his bizarre confession revealed more of himself than any of the other men or women; yet his own words must be measured against the complexity of his personality and the intricate web of events he helped to weave. Let us turn our attention first to the other men.

Compared to the frenzy of spring, the autumn interrogations proceeded at a more leisurely pace. During the first phase of the trial, the magistrates questioned fifteen men in sixty-four separate sessions, most of them conducted in the three weeks between the first arrest (27 March) and the interruption of the trial (21 April). Inflamed by the passion of the crime, it seemed, the magistrates rushed at first to extract confessions. But then, with their passion for justice and vengeance tempered by the first wave of executions in June, the magistrates, as the weather turned cold and phlegmatic, took their time with the other prisoners. Between 25 October 1475 and 11 January 1476, the magistrates interrogated six men in fifty-four separate sessions, including seventeen sessions for Israel the painter.

Leaving aside Israel's interrogations for the time being, we can detect patterns in the judicial examination of the other five men. Concluded well before Christmas, the interrogations, through the usual application of torture, coerced confessions from the men that established their subordinate roles in the official ritual murder story. If we compare these confessions, contradictory motifs begin to emerge, a tension representing the conflict between the narrative imperative dictated by torture and the confusion in the men's own stories.

For the men under torture, the trial represented a bewildering if not completely random application of violence. Put to the rope, the men simply did not know what to say. For example, on 27 October, Isaac, Engel's cook, was interrogated by the podestà; in the words of the scribe: "He [Isaac] was hoisted up, set down, and asked. He answered, Yes, if I knew what I should say, I would gladly say it. Then, after he had sat for a while and said nothing, it was ordered to pull him up."[3] Two days later, on the rope again, "[Isaac] said he wanted to tell the truth later and knew nothing and knew only that he must die."[4] Or, take the example of Lazarus, Engel's servant. Questioned on 20 November, Lazarus "was asked to repeat all that was spoken and done with the child. He answered he did not know what was said or done, as he had already said so before. Then the podestà told him, he was a fool who did not want to tell the truth, when the other imprisoned Jews have said it."[5] With respect to blood and word symbolism, the central motifs in the trial record, the Jews were at first ignorant of the lines they were supposed to say. Thus, Moses the tutor, called Young Moses, maintained he did not know what words were spoken during Simon's killing or that Jews needed Christian blood.[6] Likewise, Moses of Bamberg expressed confusion and ignorance in response to similar questions on 8 November.[7]

Joaff suffered the most. Interrogating him on 26 October, the podestà at first did not use the rope:

He was asked whether he saw the murdered boy.

JOAFF: In the ditch.
PODESTÀ: Think again.
JOAFF: In the antechamber of the synagogue.
PODESTÀ: Anywhere else?
JOAFF: No.

He was ordered stripped, tied by the rope, and hoisted up.

JOAFF: Let me down, I'll speak the truth.
PODESTÀ: Speak it on the ropes.
JOAFF: I have never done anything evil.

He was hoisted up and dropped.
He swore by his death, which he will soon suffer, that he is innocent; he has never seen the child anywhere. . . .
He did not see the child anywhere else [besides in the ditch], he would love to have seen it [elsewhere] with his own eyes.
He was hoisted up again. . . .

JOAFF: I saw the dead boy in the synagogue.
PODESTÀ: Where in the synagogue? On which day?
JOAFF: Saturday night.

But since he did not say where [in the synagogue], he was hoisted up and dropped.

JOAFF: Let me down, I will say the truth.

The podestà went up to ask him.

JOAFF: Oh my poor children and wife!

He was hoisted up again and questioned.

JOAFF: Let me down because I will say the truth.

He was let down and asked where he saw [the child] in the synagogue. He said on a bench. Then he was unbound and sent back to prison.[8]

Even after Joaff's confession, the magistrates were not satisfied. For the Jews, so the reasoning went, ignorance was simply pretense, for their rituals and folkways were inherently evil. The following day, after confessing to the details of the official story of ritual murder, Joaff protested that he was not learned; ignorant of the prayers and blessings, "he could only drive a wagon." In response, the podestà demanded "how does he know what he knows" and threatened more torture.[9]

Like aimless signs circling the torture chamber, the words of the men echoed the repeated cycles of official questions and orders. The only coherent and truthful stories they told were fragments of their own lives: detailed descriptions of daily life in the three households on the eve of the disaster that befell the Jewish community after Passover; memories of conversations, gestures, and anxieties expressed by the men who had died and the women who were still imprisoned; remembrances of places and faces from the past, real people who populated the fictive tales of past ritual murders extorted under torture; and finally, expressions of despair, in the certain knowledge of death, by men who concocted tales about the death of some Christian boy, while silent about their own lives. Still, we must be grateful for these moments when the men spoke about themselves; however inadequate, they provide the only material for an indication of the prisoners' emotional states during the trial, for a reconstruction of the lives of the Jews and the terror that engulfed their community.

The coherent story was of course the official story. Four central motifs constituted a sort of narrative imperative:

1. the confirmation of the official ritual murder story in all its details through a new set of confessions and narrative elaboration;
2. the investigation into the roles of the Jewish women, hence the creation of a gendered discourse of ritual murder;
3. the explication of Jewish rituals, in particular the uses of Christian blood and the meaning of Hebrew curses; and finally,

4. the invention of past child killings as evidence for a history of ritual murders.

The strappada extracted confirmation of the expected official story: thus Joaff confessed, in stages and broken statements, first to witnessing the killing of Simon, then to his own participation in the bloodletting;[10] both Lazarus and Moses of Bamberg repeated the details of the official version on 27 November.[11] Young Moses confessed to the official story the next day;[12] Isaac confessed his own "role" on 16 December;[13]

Were the women guilty? Did they participate in the killing, and if so, in which ritual roles? In pursuing answers to these questions, the magistrates were writing, one may say, a gendered discourse of ritual murder. All five men were asked about the extent of the women's participation: Young Moses admitted seeing the women —Brunetta, Schönlein, Sara, Süsslein, and Brünnlein—in the synagogue;[14] Isaac, Joaff, and Lazarus all maintained that the women were not present;[15] Moses of Bamberg specifically denied the women's involvement in the killing, although he claimed that they did prepare the matzo and that some knew of the impending slaughter.[16] The testimonies shielded the women to a certain extent. At most, they could be accused only of foreknowledge of the alleged murder. The separation of gender in Jewish worship led to a gendered ritual murder discourse, providing more protection for the women, whose testimonies will be examined in chapter ten.

In addition to confirming the official story, the five men also invented details of the imagined ritual killing, in response to the judicial interest in Jewish rituals. For the Christian magistrates, the alleged murder of Simon was not an ordinary crime. Merely establishing the motive and manner of the murder was insufficient; the magistrates wanted the investigation into Simon's death to unlock the secret door of Judaism and allow them to construct an ethnography of Jewish rites.

On 14 November, the podestà asked Isaac, who was hanging on the rope, to describe the "scene" in the synagogue. The scribe recorded this dialogue:

PODESTÀ: Tell all the gestures of the Jews.
ISAAC: He cannot mimic the laughter and the joy then because now he feels sad and depressed.
PODESTÀ: He does not care whether he mimics with a sad or joyous heart.
ISAAC: He laughed and said "hän, hän" or "hey, hey" . . . and made other gestures that one cannot write down, since he spoke with a crooked mouth or whispered.[17]

Gestures beyond words. Thus under torture Joaff confessed to biting the boy Simon;[18] Young Moses described a scene of jubilation, with stamping of feet and laughter;[19] still others confessed to indecent and grotesque bodily gestures, exposing their penises and bare bottoms and sticking their tongues out, all done to scorn the Christian child.[20]

The Christian child was synonymous with the Christ child. In fact, "blasphemies against Christianity" expressed the very essence of Judaism, according to the ritual murder discourse. Time and again, the podestà demanded from his prisoners the exact Hebrew prayers spoken over the child and their meanings.[21] Hans von Fundo, the scribe, notated carefully all the curses against the Holy Family,[22] including Lazarus's words: "He [Lazarus] said Jews uttered all sorts of blasphemies against Joseph, calling him a priest, Mary a whore, and Jesus, the hanged one . . . That Jesus was born from an adulterous affair between Mary and Joseph, a priest, and that Samuel told them that Simon was also born out of wedlock like Jesus."[23]

In the ethnography represented in the trial record, the vulgarity of Jewish customs was only exceeded by their barbarism: the use of human blood. Under torture, Young Moses, Isaac, Lazarus, and Moses of Bamberg confessed to drinking Simon's blood.[24] Drawn from the veins of a Christian boy martyr, collected in cups, dried into powder, and sprinkled on Seder wine and matzo, the human blood branded the Jews as inhuman in the eyes of the magistrates. Yet the authorities found the confessions satisfying. During the interrogation of Moses of Bamberg on 14 November, the following scene transpired:

> As he was hanging, the podestà asked him whether he was terrified of the discovery [of the kidnapping]. He said no, he was happy.
>
> PODESTÀ: Why?
> MOSES: Because they would scorn the Christian God.
>
> After hanging for a while longer, he said further that he felt happy because he was going to eat blood. After that he was let down.[25]

In the end, the magistrates condemned the Jews, as in the sentence pronounced over Isaac, "as Bloodeater and drinker, and blasphemer of the holiest passion of Jesus Christ His Godly Majesty and the Most Praised Virgin Mary."[26] Drinking human blood was a practice the Church frequently attributed to heretics and witches. In 1427, Bernardino of Siena preached against a secret sect alleged to be heretics and its rites in Piedmont; he accused the members of killing a little boy, pulverizing his body, and drinking the resulting mixture of powder and potion.[27] For the magistrates, cannibalism was surely a demonic inspiration, characteristic of Jews and witches.

Mere description does not establish ethnographic authority; the ethnographer must act the part of historian, probing into the origins of the rites and customs he purports to describe. The magistrates confronted Moses of Bamberg with both their historic and ethnographic authority. The podestà forced Moses to admit to the killing on 14 November. Still hanging from the rope, Moses

> said he wishes his head had been cut off, rather than this should come to pass that Jews had killed the child.

PODESTÀ: Why?
MOSES: Now that the news is out Jews kill Christians for blood and to scorn Jesus, the whole world will hate Jews.

A little later:

MOSES: This Jewish custom of eating Christian blood has been a secret.
PODESTÀ: We Christians have known for a long time—it is in books. It has often been talked about publicly.
MOSES: It might have been said among Christians but not all believed it, but now all Trent Jews have confessed to this, and all would believe it. That is why he would rather have his head chopped off than to have what happened happened and to have the murder exposed.[28]

Then, tortured into admitting previous ritual murders, Moses named cases, both from hearsay and fabricated from his own past. Twelve years before in Bayreuth, he said, he drank blood purchased from one Salomon; nine years earlier, while transporting merchandise to Frankfurt-an-der-Oder, a different Salomon and Jakob, his traveling companions, killed a child in the woods; Jews trafficked in Christian blood, peddling their wares with certificates issued by their rabbis; he also told of a ritual murder trial in Alsace that took place a short time before (referring to Endingen in 1470), when some Jews were burned, while others fled after the discovery of partially decomposed bodies in the Christian ossuary and the immediate charge of ritual murder.[29] And so, the real and the imaginary fused into a seamless whole; the lies Moses told under duress only confirmed the veracity of the historic Endingen trial which became, in turn, the fulcrum of the fictive universe of Jewish violence.

Every one of the Jews was tortured until he narrated a history of ritual murders. Joaff told the podestà on 27 October that for sixteen years he had been servant to Mayer in Würzburg; this Mayer had told him all about the need for Christian blood, just as he was now telling the podestà. A Christian maid, Elsa Baumgartner, who cleaned Mayer's house every Sabbath, smuggled three Christian children into the house, where the cook Seligman killed them over prayers. The podestà questioned Joaff at length about this alleged Würzburg murder: When did it occur? (Four years earlier) How was the body disposed of? Who were the children? Were Mayer and Seligman still alive? Joaff admitted that two years before while he was in Ansbach, he had heard that they were still alive.[30]

Thus Young Moses confessed to knowledge of an alleged ritual murder, committed by Mayer Pibman in his home in Nuremberg eight years earlier, and that for the entire ten years Young Moses was in Nuremberg he drank blood.[31] Likewise, Lazarus, Engel's servant, said that while in the castle Seraval, in the territory of the Truchsess, he first heard of the use of blood from his father, Aaron; his uncle, Ritzard, once told his father and Engel of an alleged child murder in Regensburg.[32] And Isaac, also Engel's servant, said that, in a perverted representation of Jewish charity, rich Jews give poor Jews Christian blood without charge.[33] He also mentioned the Endingen trial; four or five years before, a Jew was burned for bringing Christian blood to Pforzheim, in the territory of the Count of Württemberg.[34] Pressed for more historical facts, he said: fifteen years before, when he was a schoolboy in Worms, forty Jews bought a child from a beggar woman and killed him at Passover. More recently, he had heard from Engel that Ritzard, a Jew in Brixen, took some blood from the Christian child who was killed in Regensburg.[35]

Moses of Bamberg heard his confessions read aloud and translated into German for his consent on 27 November. He swore on his Hebrew oath that his story was true. Three days later, the prison guard found him dead in his cell, as a result of torture or suicide, we do not know. Nevertheless, the podestà sentenced his corpse to be dragged to the execution ground to be burned post mortem.[36]

On 14 December, Lazarus heard his confession read back to

him. He changed a few minor statements. But when the podestà asked him to swear to it in Hebrew, he refused, saying it was a sin to swear. Despite repeated demands, Lazarus was adamant. "At that the podestà said," in the words of the scribe, "if all the aforementioned things that he has confessed to and confirmed are true, he has no choice but to swear on the Hebrew Scriptures, by the name of the living, true God who created heaven and earth, in accordance with Jewish customs. He answered, he would not swear. He was asked why. He answered, it would be a sin. And as often the podestà repeated, since it is true it would not be a sin to swear, since one is swearing to the truth, he insisted he would not swear because it would be a sin."[37] Sending him back to his cell, the podestà and others later visited Lazarus at the first hour at night. Somehow, perhaps by threat of more torture, they got Lazarus to swear an oath in Hebrew, if we trust the trial record.[38] The logic of the torture chamber was contested until the bitter end.

Isaac heard his confession read back to him in German on 20 December. He consented and swore the required oath.[39] The procedure was repeated on the same day with Young Moses, as it had been with Joaff on 11 December.[40]

Sentencing would come with the new year.

It cannot be emphasized enough that the Trent blood libel represented the central link in a long chain of events, thanks to the intervention of the papacy and the bitter polemics it aroused. Other trials preceded it, others followed. In the southern German-Alpine region, many rumors and accusations of Jewish child murders poisoned the atmosphere, as we can reconstruct from the trial record and other sources associated with the trial:

1430 Ravensburg: Several Jews were executed when a dead child was discovered in the cellar of their house.
1440 Meran: A Christian planted a dead child in the house of a Jew, but the plot was uncovered by the captain of the town.

1440 Landshut: Fifty-five Jews were burned on a ritual murder charge.

1461 Trent: Blond Gretchen's missing son was found in Samuel's shed.

1461 Pfullendorf: Jews were condemned to death for alleged child murder.

1470 Endingen: Jews were accused of the alleged murder of a Christian family and burned to death.

1473 Trent: When the body of the missing Eysenposch child was found, Bishop Hinderbach ordered it to be examined for cut marks.

1475 Regensburg: rumors of a blood libel in the town reached the Jews of Brixen.

These cases represented *real* persecutions, in addition to the many more *imagined* past ritual slaughters, extracted from the Jews through torture. If we construct a cultural geography of blood libel in the region, Trent would appear at the southernmost tip. In short, the location of ritual murder trials coincided with the boundary of German settlements in the Alpine Highlands. Prior to the Trent trial of 1475, the numerous Jewish communities in the Veneto and Lombardy were spared the terror of ritual murder trials. To use the words of Israel the painter spoken under torture, "Although the Germans say Jews kill Christian children, it is simply not true."[41]

The four motifs analyzed above—official story, gendered discourse, distortion of Jewish rituals, and the invention of past ritual murder—bring us to the functions of the narrative imperative. To put it another way, what was the meaning of the confessions, suggested by official questioning and extracted under torture? The most obvious was the literal meaning of the trial record: the confessions, as part of the judicial proceedings, confirmed *post factum* the previous executions in June and legitimated sentencing and execution of the five men. This literal meaning, however, represented merely the core of a larger structure of symbols. A second, more diffuse level of meaning is represented by the creation of a genealogy or history of ritual murders that connected present and past. Understood in this context, the trial in Trent was not conducted on the whim of prince-bishop and his magistrates but as a historical link in the unfolding of "Jewish evil." And finally, a larger field of symbols encompasses the first two symbolic structures: both the Trentino "present" and the "history" of Jewish crimes represent the Christian conception of the practices inherent in Jewish life and ritual. The very essence of Jewish rites, the magistrates carefully reconstructed from the Seder meal, the Haggadah, and blood symbolism, demanded the sacrifice of Christian boys. Thus, the unique event, Simon's death, and the historicity of past child murders are subsumed in the eternal structure of repeated Jewish rituals. And the narrative imperative, the official story of ritual murder, the trial record of 1475–76, represents nothing less than a Christian ethnography of Jewish rites.

CHAPTER NINE

THE CONVERT

I srael, the twenty-three-year-old son of Mayer of Brandenburg, made a living copying Hebrew books, illuminating them with gold and color tints. Widely traveled, searching for work and adventure, he ended his journey in Trent. Israel was tortured, like the others, after he was arrested while fleeing the city. On 21 April, the day when Sigismund temporarily suspended the trial, Israel asked for baptism, hoping to escape execution. Baptized Wolfgang, he was released from his cell but kept within the Buonconsiglio, as a living demonstration of Christian justice and charity.[1]

After the arrests, the magistrates confiscated all Jewish properties. In early June, before the resumption of the trial and the first executions, Hinderbach decided to liquidate part of the Jewish assets so that the material objects, taken as pledges for loans, were to be returned to the debtors. Someone had to go through the Hebrew registers and letters; on 8 June, Israel was appointed to oversee the return of the pledges.[2] The task completed, he was released and received permission to earn a living by changing money.[3] During the summer months, Israel, or Wolfgang as he was now known, even gained the confidence of the episcopal entourage and enjoyed access to the Buonconsiglio. In fact, the convert was playing a dangerous game, trying to ingratiate himself with his new masters while helping to free the imprisoned Jewish women and children. Whether out of circumstance or bad conscience, he became the contact for Venetian Jews who were organizing a rescue effort. During the apostolic commissioner's sojourn in Trent, Israel acted as a valuable informant. He might even have been involved in a bizarre plot to poison Hinderbach. All this came to light when Israel was rearrested on 27 October, after the other Jews named him in their confessions as one of the participants in the Passover Seder. Perhaps his clandestine dealings had already betrayed him to the authorities. In any event, over the next ten weeks, during seventeen interrogation sessions, Israel told a story of intrigues and plots, and of cowardice and courage.

The first interrogation took place on 2 November. After telling the podestà the circumstances of his arrival in Trent, Israel disclaimed any personal knowledge of the alleged ritual killing. Transferred to the torture chamber, he cried out on the rope: "Oh Jesus, I am innocent, I pray that the martyr would perform a miracle, as I am innocent!"[4] After a while, Israel admitted to seeing the child on the almemor; he claimed he was terrified, got angry, and left the synagogue. "Why did he not say the truth before?" asked the podestà. Israel answered, "He feared for his life." The podestà then questioned him as to the reason, manner, and timing of the alleged ritual murder. The scribe noted that Israel "gave different answers to the question."[5] Under further torture, he eventually "described" Simon's death but insisted that he did not take part in the killing, which, as he told the podestà, terrified him.[6]

Interrogated the next day, Israel continued to play the role of the cooperative convert. He explained the various uses of Christian blood in Jewish ceremonies, described the Hebrew curses, and told his tormentors "we [the Christians] cannot write the words correctly; if it pleases the podestà, he would write down the Hebrew and German."[7] After a short break, the interrogations resumed. The podestà was now interested in other child killings. Israel fabricated four incidents to satisfy his tormentors: one murder fourteen years earlier in Günzenhausen, another committed by Abraham of Feltre, one in Plebissach near Padua four to five years before the Trent trial, and a recent case in Wending.[8]

For the next two weeks, the magistrates were busy examining the five other men. Israel next appeared in the torture chamber on 16 November. He was asked various questions concerning Simon's death and the fictitious child murders to which he had confessed knowledge.[9]

Israel underwent a long torture session on 18 November. After Israel had described more details of the imagined ritual killing of Simon, the podestà asked for further information on other child murders. At first, Israel claimed he had only heard about these charges but had no first-hand knowledge. Convinced he was lying, the podestà ordered more severe torture. Israel broke down. He invented a story about Regensburg which would have grave consequences for that Jewish community. The scribe recorded this confession: eight years earlier in Regensburg, when Israel was staying with Samuel, a Jew named Jossel bought a Christian child from a beggar for ten ducats before Passover. On Passover, some twenty-five or twenty-six Jews, including himself, stuck the boy with needles and used his blood for their ceremonies. He named fourteen Regensburg Jews: Hirsch, Sayar alias Straubingen, Mayer Heller, Gutkind, Mayer Pawman, Eberlin, Tall Jacob, Isaac, Ritzard of Brixen, Rabbi Jossel, Bozzel Thoz, Simon Hattlaz, Samuel Kalbskopff, and Gossel Fursinger.[10]

In the first months of 1476, Bishop Heinrich of Regensburg,

with whom Hinderbach was in correspondence regarding the trial, obtained a copy of Israel's confession when he passed through Trent on his return from Rome. Upon Bishop Heinrich's return to his diocese, the imaginary killing and the names remembered under torture became the basis for a ritual murder investigation in Regensburg. Most of the men named by Israel were arrested, along with others; all the prisoners were interrogated under torture; several of them confessed. Before the Regensburg magistrates could execute the Jews, Emperor Friedrich III intervened; as subjects of the Imperial Chamber, the Jews were directly under his command, so the emperor reminded the magistrates of the imperial city. After a long impasse—punctuated by petitions, mandates, and protestations—the Regensburgers released the Jews on 4 September 1480, four and a half years after their arrest.[11]

Israel's spectacular confession intensified magisterial interest in other alleged ritual murders. During the next two interrogations (20 and 22 November), the podestà asked him whether Christian children had been killed in Bozen, Meran, or Innsbruck.[12] As Israel retraced his wanderings, he offered the podestà stories of ritual murders, created by his imagination and peopled with names from his memory. Thus, Ritzard of Brixen, who had paid him one ducat to copy and illuminate Hebrew books, in the tale procured blood from Regensburg.[13] While staying in Abraham's house in Feltre, Israel had heard that a child was killed in Mestre near Venice; for the benefit of the podestà, Abraham became the culprit.[14]

Next, the podestà questioned Israel's connections to the apostolic commissioner. For two days (22 and 23 November), Israel recounted a long story of his secret contacts with Venetian Jews and the bishop of Ventimiglia during September and October in an effort to contact the Jewish women and secure their release.[15] This was his story:

> When the apostolic commissioner arrived in Trent, he was accompanied by Salomon, who had a safe conduct from Sigismund.

This Salomon sought out Israel, gave him one ducat, and promised five more if Israel would agree to meet with a notary. Israel agreed. Salomon then introduced him to an one-eyed notary who came with the apostolic commission. The one-eyed man wanted to know everything that was said and done in the Buonconsiglio, especially the tortures. A meeting was arranged. Late at night, under the cover of darkness, the notary brought Israel into the inn where the apostolic commissioner was staying. In a room, Israel found three men, the bishop-legate, the priest Raphael, and an old man. The one-eyed notary served as interpreter, since Israel spoke no Italian, and the bishop no German. The bishop of Ventimiglia asked whether the Jews actually killed the child and how they were tortured. Israel replied that he was tortured, with rope, onion, and boiled eggs. The legate wanted to talk to the Jewish women, but Israel warned them that the women were heavily guarded. The bishop of Ventimiglia gave Israel fifty ducats and asked him to tell the women the legate would help to set them free. The bishop also said he was leaving Trent for Rovereto and then Rome, but Israel could contact him in Rovereto through Salomon. The priest Raphael wrote down the conversation. Since the bishop of Ventimiglia left Trent on the twenty-third of September, the meeting probably took place a few days before that.

Almost a month passed. Then, on 19 October, eight days before his arrest, Israel got up from his money counter (*Wechselbank*) to go to lunch when he noticed someone was following him. The stranger asked Israel whether he recognized him. Israel said no. The stranger then introduced himself as Hans Peter of Monta, a baptized Jew; the two of them had been traveling companions in Nuremberg six or seven years earlier, before their conversion. Israel then recognized him. The acquaintances talked on. Hans Peter told Israel he was sick and had come to worship the dead boy martyr. The next day, Hans Peter came to Israel at the shop. He wanted to talk to the Jewish women, who were under house arrest and a strong guard. Israel said he did not want to have anything to do with the matter. Two days later, Israel ran into Hans Peter, who now confided in Israel that he was sent by the Jews in Rovereto to contact the women—some of them were relatives of the Trent families, now pleading their case with the

bishop of Ventimiglia. Again, Israel declined involvement. Later in
the day, he met Hans Peter and told him finally that Brünnlein,
Samuel's widow, was confined to Engel's house; Hans Peter could
talk to her through the window. The following day, Hans Peter
came to report. Yes, he had followed Israel's advice and managed
to talk to Brünnlein. He had asked her whether the women had
been tortured. At this point, Israel spontaneously admitted he
himself was put to the rack and had onion held under his nose.
Hans Peter said that the Jews heard that the men and women in
Trent were now given some provisions, but that the Jews executed in June had been severely tortured.[16]

To the podestà, Israel was a double Judas: he had betrayed both
Simon and Bishop Hinderbach. Giovanni de Salis probably felt
contempt for this Jew-Christian, thinking perhaps of the many
nasty proverbs about converts ("It is difficult to teach converts
and dogs new tricks. . . .")[17] For Israel, baptism did not spare
him repeated tortures, and Simon had performed no miracles to
prove his innocence. Terrified of death, Israel became the convert
Wolfgang and renounced his past. Yet, pricked by his conscience,
he could not deny the injustice nor ignore the plight of the
imprisoned women. Oscillating between the different roles demanded of him, Israel was alternatively the wandering Jew, the
Christian convert, informant to the apostolic commissioner, and
the cooperative prisoner. But for once, in anger, he tore off his
mask. During the interrogation of 23 November, Israel admitted
the reason for his conversion: when he was first arrested, he
feared he would die and thus asked to be baptized. He revealed
himself in these words, as recorded by the scribe:

> PODESTÀ: What did he think of the Christian faith?
> ISRAEL: He wants to say the truth. He does not believe in anything
> of the Christian faith. . . It is a joke to say that God came down
> from heaven to earth, walked around and lived among men. He
> believes only in God and nothing more. He believes also that the
> Jewish faith is right and holy.
> PODESTÀ: Does he believe that it is right, according to Jewish law,

that Jews kill Christian children and drink and eat their blood as
he himself had said.

ISRAEL: He believes firmly that it is right that Jews kill Christian
children and eat their blood. He wants to have Christian blood at
Easter, even now that he is baptized he wants to die a Jew.[18]

Powerless to strike back at his tormentors, Israel defiantly affirmed the myth of ritual murder, the only weapon of the weak.

Like a flash of lightning, Israel's defiant rage illuminated his
self, then, just as quickly it vanished, returning us to the dark
opaqueness of the torture chamber. One week after his outburst
(30 November), Israel, apparently not under torture, as the scribe
tells us, recounted the official story of Simon's death.[19] On 6
December, he explained that the various tortures were meant to
mimic the crucifixion.[20]

To tarnish his name, the magistrates painted Israel as a petty
thief. During the session of 17 December, with Count von Terlaco
translating and Peter Rauter transcribing, Israel confessed to lar-
ceny. In September, he had stolen on many occasions from the
pawned goods being inventoried in the houses that used to belong
to Samuel, Tobias, and Engel—small items all, pearls, silver and
gold figurines, cups, and plates. When arrested in October, he
gave the things to Hans, the tower guard, for safekeeping. Hans
claimed all the things were still in the sack that Israel had given
him. He went to fetch the sack and every item described was
found.[21] Israel also confessed to stealing some clothes in the castle
and handing them over to the cook, Anna.[22]

If the story of petty thievery is credible—after all, the items
rightfully belonged to the Jewish families and Israel was simply
taking what he needed for himself—then the subsequent confession of poison revealed more than anything the paranoia of Hinderbach's court. The next day (18 December), Israel was tortured
into confessing to an elaborate plot to poison Bishop Hinderbach,
the podestà, and the captain. As Israel told his story: One day in
September, he saw some powder in the chancery. Masters Georg

and Nicholas, notaries, were there and told Israel it was poison. It was unclear how the poison got to the chancery, but the notaries thought that Master Peter, an illuminator, had left it in his trunk when he left Trent. With nobody looking, Israel stole some powder and showed it to Salomon. This Salomon was trying to persuade Sigismund to release the Jews; he seemed pessimistic because the archduke wanted to find out whether the Jews were guilty. Israel had first met Salomon through Caspar, a German servant to Sigismund's Undermarschall. Sometime in September, Caspar came to Israel's money shop and indicated that Salomon wanted to talk to him. Twice, Israel and Salomon communicated secretly through Caspar; both times they met in the stable of the inn where Salomon was staying. According to Israel, Salomon asked him to spy on things in the castle, particularly Hinderbach's daily routine, and to poison him, perhaps putting poison in his wine or food. Failing that, he could poison the well in the Buonconsiglio.[23]

An often-repeated charge against the Jews, well-poisoning became a commonplace in anti-Jewish discourse after the plague epidemics of the mid-fourteenth century. On one hand, the accusation against Israel was likely to have been fabricated in order to harm the reputation of the Jews who were trying to free the imprisoned women. On the other, Hinderbach and his courtiers could very well have believed in a real plot against their lives. In Renaissance Italy, poison was widely used to dispose of enemies; the princely courts furnished enough examples. But less exalted persons also resorted to poison, as in the case of a Florentine woman who obtained poison from a Jewish physician to murder her husband; both met their death when the plot came to light.[24] Perhaps Hinderbach was thinking of a vendetta against him. In any event, fear of poison pervaded the episcopal entourage. After the charge against Israel, another "poison plot" was uncovered in March 1476, when the podestà accused Paolo di Novara, a priest who transcribed several copies of the trial proceedings, of conspiracy. Under judicial torture, Paolo confessed to working in collusion with the Jews of Lombardy and Venice to poison Hinderbach.[25]

The podestà asked Israel more questions about Salomon on 21 December[26] after which the trial adjourned for Christmas. The proceedings began again with the new year, on 10 January, when the podestà offered Israel an advocate, following established legal procedure. Israel chose Hans Maria von Lippis, although he knew it would not matter in the end whom he chose.[27] After confirming some details of Israel's previous confessions, the podestà swore in Hans Maria as advocate for the young Jew on 11 January.[28]

Israel was brought before the bench of law in the Buonconsiglio on 15 January. Assisting the podestà were the notary, Hans Hellgruber of Bozen, and Hans von Fundo, the law clerk; von Fundo translated Israel's confessions back to him in German. Correcting a few minor mistakes, Israel swore to the confession. Then, a last outburst: "Just before he was led out, he cried out in German to the podestà. The Devil gave him the idea to do all these things; and now he realizes he must die for them. However, he begged [the podestà] to be merciful and sentence him to a quick death so that he would soon die. After it was translated for him, the podestà said he would consider the petition and urged Wolfgang to seek consolation in Christ."[29] And so, Israel played out his last public role, as the demonic Jew turned Christian apostate.

The new year opened with executions. On the thirteenth of January, the podestà sentenced Lazarus and Isaac to the gallows, "to be strung up with a length of rope around the neck until [their] souls depart from the body, and the bodies are to be left there forever."[30] Two days later, Israel was sentenced to be broken on the wheel and burned; Joaff and Young Moses were sentenced to be hanged.[31] Joaff and Moses asked for baptism and in return received what was considered a less painful death. The Dominican Heinrich of Schlestett baptized Joaff as Anthony and Moses as Marcello.

The gallows were set up outside St. Martin's Gate, only a short distance from the Buonconsiglio. A crowd gathered on 16 January for the spectacle of Christian triumph.[32] The imperial notary, Odoric Wilhelm of Brescia, who recorded the proceedings for the court, named many illustrious Trentini as being present: the Dominican Heinrich of Schlettstett, professor of sacred theology; Peter Schrec, chaplain and rector of the cathedral school; Herman Schindelar, one time chamberlain of the prince-bishop; Master Michael; Nicholas, called Langmontol of Trameno; Berthold of Burgo; Jochel of Sterzing and other pilgrims from Rome, among many others. Johannes Wiser, canon of the cathedral and acting vicar of Bishop Hinderbach, addressed the two prisoners, who were hanging from the gallows with their feet just touching the platform. Wiser asked whether they had been baptized and intended to die in the faith of Christ. They replied yes. Then each in turn recited the articles of faith, the Apostles' Creed, the Lord's Prayer, and gave a general confession. Johannes Wiser exhorted both to persist in their faith, to put their trust in Christ and the Virgin Mary, to reflect on the brevity of life on earth and eternal salvation. Dutifully, the prisoners invoked the names of Christ and Mary. Stating they and the other Jews had been condemned on account of the murder of Simon, Wiser asked "the innocent boy" to intercede on their behalf before God. Both men affirmed their guilt and asked for the intercession of "the boy and his innocent blood," so that omnipotent God might forgive their sins. And when all was said and recorded, Joaff and Moses met their end.

On 19 January, Israel was dragged to the same execution ground. Broken on the wheel, he was burned as "a thief, eater and drinker of Christian blood, poisoner, blasphemer, traitor, and an enemy of Christ and Godly majesty."[33]

CHAPTER TEN

THE WOMEN

Besides the expected confessions extracted under torture, the testimonies of the Jewish women revealed much about their lives, both before and after the disaster that destroyed their families. They told about conditions of their house arrest and how they received help from Christian neighbors. Their testimonies allow us to reconstruct the web of relationships and behavior that constituted the three Jewish households, particularly, their own gender roles within the small community. In short, their confessions represented as much a gendered discourse of ritual murder as fragmentary narratives about the lives of Jewish women.

One of the demands of the apostolic commissioner was that the women and children be set free. Johannes Hinderbach, however, refused to comply despite Dei Giudici's insistence. For the Trentini, the women were not only witnesses to the "crime"; they were also potential hostile witnesses who could undermine the legitimacy of the trial if released into the custody of the apostolic commissioner. As we have seen, the Jewish communities in the Veneto tried to contact the women through Israel the painter and other intermediaries. If it was too late to rescue the men, at least the women and children could still be saved from death or forced baptism.

After the arrest of the men, the authorities kept the women and children under house arrest as they prepared to proceed against them. During November 1475, the magistrates began interrogating Sara and Schönlein, came under heavy criticism in Rome, postponed the trial, and only resumed in March 1476. Altogether the magistrates conducted twenty-six interrogations. The podestà wanted to interrogate all the women during the fall of 1475, but the physicians strongly advised against putting the sick women under torture.[1] Süsslein, or Dulceta, was suffering from a serious case of dropsy and died in January 1476; Brünnlein (Engel's mother), Gütlein (Engel's sister), and Anna (Israel's widow and Samuel's daughter-in-law) all suffered from prolonged fevers—the latter two were only questioned after their recovery in the spring of 1476. So in the end, only Sara (Tobias' widow) and Schönlein (Mayer's widow) were interrogated during the final months of 1475, with Gütlein and Anna questioned the following spring.

Gender dictated the authorities' dealings with the women. At the first hearing against Sara (3 November), undertaken in a room of the Buonconsiglio, the podestà wanted to ascertain if Sara could legally be put to torture. As she was being led away from a session during which she recalled in detail the events preceding the arrest but denied ever having seen Simon, the podestà interrupted. Through an interpreter, he asked whether Sara was pregnant. She answered, in German, that "she had not suffered her illness [menstruation] after the departure of her husband. Her body has also gotten bigger. But she does not know for certain whether she is pregnant."[2] Did Sara know that the common criminal codes in the Empire forbade the interrogation of pregnant women under torture? In any event, it did not help her. The next day, 4 November, she was brought to the podestà's house. There a midwife, the wife of Master Caspar Goldschmid, examined her. The result was negative, as the notary Hans von Lasia duly recorded.[3] Sara was then introduced to the torture chamber in the castle.

Was the cessation of menstruation a symptom of a deeper malaise?[4] A young woman of twenty-five, Sara was at the prime child-bearing age. Could it be that her bodily disorder reflected the larger disintegration of her world? Her family torn apart, her husband brutally executed, her children released from house arrest, now her body refused to follow its natural course. As is well documented in the medical literature, the cessation of menses could result from a severe psychic shock or from incarceration and malnutrition; moreover, significant abdominal distention can also occur in this circumstance, hence Sara's apparently pregnant appearance.[5] According to her own words in the trial record, Sara contrasted her present disorder to the biological and ritual order of former, happier days. Sara told the podestà she customarily cleansed herself in the ritual bath in Samuel's house after each menstrual period. After her arrival in Trent and marriage to Tobias, she had gone there three or four times for the ritual cleansing; the last time was only two or three days before Passover.[6] After the arrest, of course, her menstruation had stopped.

The biological cycle interrupted, nature and body in disarray —the connection with the trial was made explicit by Schönlein. She told the podestà she had heard that Christian blood "cured" menstruation. She, however, never drank it except at Passover, for "she had never been pregnant in her eighteen years [of marriage] and had never had menstrual flow since the same time."[7] Schönlein was perhaps lying to save herself, for the blood libel attributed every power to Christian blood, including the power to "cure" the menstruation of Jewish women. Asserting she had not had menstrual flow for eighteen years meant she had never partaken of Christian blood. In her narrative, Schönlein thus suppressed her own bodily nature to conform with Christian projections of Jewish superstitions.[8]

If the women's bodies represented one motif in their confessions, life-cycle was another prominent theme. All four women described their successive stages in life, as daughters, young spouses, widows, and mothers. Thus Sara remembered herself as a girl in her father's household, then a young bride of thirteen or fourteen, widowed at twenty, and married again, to Tobias, at twenty-four mother and stepmother to four children.[9] Schönlein described herself as the daughter of Seligman and Gütlein of Nuremberg, the wife of Mayer at sixteen, first living with her in-laws, then with Samuel's household in Trent.[10] Gütlein told of her childhood, of life with her mother and stepfather, the frequent moves, her unhappy marriage to a gambling husband who abandoned her, her divorce, and her eventual return to the family of her mother and brother.[11] And finally, Anna, "the daughter of Abraham, son of the late Jew Lazarus of Brescia," recounted growing up in her father's house near Padua, then moving to Trent as the young bride of Israel, the son of Samuel and grandson of Seligman of Nuremberg.

The stories the women told about themselves were only of incidental interest to the magistrates. Instead, the judicial panel concentrated on three points: the confirmation of the official story of ritual murder; the determination of the degree of the women's involvement; and the investigation of whether or not and how outside messages were smuggled to the women.

Concerning the official story, the rope elicited the desired responses. True, the magistrates did not severely torture the women, as they had the men, which was due less to consideration than to the fact that they did not think the women participated in the supposed killing of Simon. Let us listen to the stories of Sara and Schönlein.

During Sara's first interrogation on 3 November, she was not tortured. The podestà questioned her repeatedly on Tobias's whereabouts on the night of the arrest. Although Sara maintained she had never seen the dead child, the podestà persisted. "Then, she clasped her hands together and said, almost on the verge of tears, it was true, she had never seen [the child]."[12] The next day (4 November) at the Buonconsiglio, her interrogation resumed:

PODESTÀ: Did she leave her house on Passover and where did she go?
SARA: Yes, she went to Samuel's house for a ritual bath when it was late.
PODESTÀ: Did she go alone?
SARA: Tobias was with her.
PODESTÀ: After they had returned home, did Tobias go out again?
SARA: She does not know; she was in the next room.

Order was given to strip and bind her, and then the same question was asked.

SARA: Tobias did not want her to see anything. He said she was too young.
PODESTÀ: What was the "thing" Tobias did not want her to see?
SARA: When Tobias cauterized waters (*Wasser ausgeprennt*) or prepared medicine, he did not want her to see.

Order was given to hoist her up.

PODESTÀ: What is it that Tobias does not want her to see? After they had returned home and he had finished eating, how long was he out?

She was given a jolt.

SARA: One to two hours, she does not know.

Ordered to hoist her up.

PODESTÀ: Speak the truth!
SARA: She does not know whether he went out. If he did, he did not tell her.

A jolt.

SARA: She will speak if they let her down. He Tobias might very well have gone out again. She does not know really what he wanted or what he was doing because she was busy in the kitchen.

She was hoisted up.

SARA: He was out for two to three hours. She was busy with housework. Sometimes she saw him, sometimes not.

She was hoisted up. She gave the same answer. She was made to jump or dance [i.e. a jolt, author's note]. She asked to be let down, she will speak the truth.

SARA: Her husband is dead, if she knows anything about him she will say it.
PODESTÀ: She should speak the truth.
SARA: She has said it.

It was ordered to hoist her up.[13]

This was the end of the first torture session.

Sara was again tortured on 5 November. After a couple of "jumps," she broke down. From then on, merely the threat of torture frightened Sara into telling the podestà what he wanted to hear. Allowed to sit on a chair, she described the Seder, the sabbath service, the blood, its uses, and the dead child on the almemor, in sum, the official story.[14]

Not quite satisfied, the podestà resumed questioning on 6 November and asked Sara who carried the dead child from the almemor. The question provoked this interchange:

SARA: She was promised yesterday that she would not be asked anymore questions. So they should stop asking.
PODESTÀ: Does she now not want to say the truth, if so, he will let her be led off and bound.
SARA: She will now say the truth, if it does not cost her her life.
PODESTÀ: She should say the truth.

He ordered her to be bound and hoisted up.

SARA: I see that you desire my death.

And as she was being led away and bound,

SARA: You want me to say something, which will result in my death.

PODESTÀ: She should speak the truth.
SARA: What did Bella, or Schönlein, confess to?
PODESTÀ: She repeated the truth.[15]

Thinking of ways to escape torture, Sara invented an ingenious fiction. She told the podestà the Jews slapped the child and asked permission to demonstrate, a maneuver that gave her arms a few minutes of rest. Then she explained the motive of ritual murder: Christians and Jews were enemies because Jews killed Christ.[16]

Schönlein was easier to break. The podestà interrogated her twice, once without torture (3 November), once with (4 November). Schönlein, however, "swore on her soul she knew nothing."[17] At the third session, she told the official story—she saw the child in the synagogue and went on to demonstrate the slappings. Untied and seated, Schönlein named the Jews present at the supposed killing and the curses. Then she asked to be dismissed because she was hungry. The podestà assured Schönlein that a good meal was being prepared for her, but she first had to speak the truth. Obligingly, Schönlein described the details of the torture; as she said Mayer had related them to her, so she told the magistrate.[18]

Sara's fifth interrogation on 17 November was the last of the year for the women.[19] Throughout November and December, the magistrates concentrated on questioning the men, especially Israel; during January, there were executions to be carried out. The interrogations of the Jewish women resumed on 4 February 1476, with two sessions for Sara and Schönlein. They were not interrogated again until early March. Meanwhile, the magistrates questioned Anna and Gütlein closely, both under torture; Gütlein was questioned five times in March, Anna, seven times. In addition to the usual questions about the alleged ritual murder of Simon, the magistrates focused on two things: other ritual murders and the visit of the apostolic commissioner.

Like their menfolk, the women invented repeated rumors of past ritual murders to escape torture. Thus on 6 March, Schönlein told of a previous child murder in Trent three years earlier; Tobias played the main role. She did not know whether the child was German or Italian; in any case, nobody reported a missing child.[20] The next day, Schönlein repeated the story, claiming she had heard it from Tobias.[21] When the magistrates asked Schönlein on 28 March for more details on this earlier alleged murder in Trent, she tried to exonerate the Jewish boys. She told the magistrates that Jewish boys were not initiated into the secret killing rituals until the age of fourteen or when they reached the age of reason; the young boys in the community would not have known of this murder.[22] Anna also repeated this ritual murder tale. On 12 and 21 March, under torture, she confessed to knowledge of a child murder in Trent three years earlier, a story she had heard from Tobias's first wife, Anna, and her in-laws. She had learned all the details of this murder from her late husband, Israel. The child, like Simon, was a peasant's boy.[23] And, for the third and final time, the story was repeated on 27 March by Gütlein, Engel's sister, who claimed she had also heard it from Tobias's late wife, Anna. Except for minor variations—the child was purchased from a Christian woman, Tobias had other servants then, and a pious woman named Miriam stayed in Trent for Passover—Gütlein's ritual murder tale replicated the official story of Simon's death in detail.[24]

Trapped in a desperate situation, the women showed subtle skills to protect themselves. Turning the gender separation in worship to their advantage, the women represented themselves primarily in their domestic roles as only partial participants in religious rites that had been perverted by the blood libel into barbaric customs. Schönlein was particularly adept. Her own role in the alleged murder, she told the magistrates, was a passive one: When she saw the child in Samuel's house, she asked Brünnlein what the men were doing with Simon. Brünnlein snapped at her: "It's none of your business. Just get supper ready and you are doing fine."[25] The gendered separation of space also provided some protection for the women. Excluded from the synagogue proper, their place was in the kitchen; hence, their role in the Seder/alleged ritual murder was confined mainly to the preparation of matzo. Food preparation, a central theme in the women's own stories, was of little importance in the official discourse of ritual murder.[26] If women were marginalized in the representa-

Figure 7. The *Eruv Hazerot*. Detail from the "Rothschild Miscellany," folio 123b. It reads: "It was customary on the eve of Passover, in the afternoon, to collect a bit of flour from every householder and make from the flour a single Matzoh for the *Eruv* (domain), so all would be included in the *Eruv*. After [it is baked], the one who is symbolically uniting the properties has someone stand next to him to hold the matzoh on behalf of the entire community" (translation by Pearl Berger). Illuminated manuscript, northern Italy, 1450–1470. Reproduced courtesy of the Israel Museum, Jerusalem.

tion of the Jewish household, they also escaped the full force of terror against the Jewish community.

As the authorities had feared, the women had succeeded in receiving messages from the apostolic commissioner during his stay in Trent. In addition to confirming the role of intermediary played by Israel, the women's stories revealed the help of sympathetic Christians, who kept alive their hope of freedom.

The arrival of the apostolic commissioner aroused great excitement. Sara heard of it from Israel, who told her that the commissioner wanted to free the women and talk to them, but Sigismund and Hinderbach were opposed. Israel tried to encourage the women but feared that they would be transferred to the castle and locked up separately. Still, Sara, having learned that Dei Giudici did not believe in all the reported miracles attributed to Simon, placed great hopes in the commissioner and shared her knowledge with Anna and Schönlein.[27]

Even before the arrival of the apostolic commissioner, the women received help from courageous Christians. Twice, Roper the tailor visited the women, talked to them from the side street through a hole in the outside wall, and told them that Salomon and the commissioner were trying to free them.[28] After the women were placed under house arrest, friends and neighbors risked punishment to smuggle in letters. Anna received a letter from Rabbi Jacob of Arck, hidden in meat and passed along by Renn Insfeld. She got another six or seven letters written by Salomon through Sophia, daughter of Master Hans the furrier. Sophia handed over the letters, hidden in baskets of eggs and spices, when the guard was not watching. The women read the letters in haste and burned them. Salomon's letters encouraged the women to take heart, for he was petitioning Sigismund for their release, and the Roman Jews had gotten a papal commission appointed to save their coreligionists in Trent. Since they lived together in Samuel's house, Anna could read the letters in secret to Sara and Schönlein. After Dei Giudici's departure, the women wrote him letters about the condition of their imprisonment.

Sophia smuggled the letters out and gave them to her father, who took them in person to Rovereto, to the commissioner.[29] Süsslein, who was under guard in Engel's house, also managed to smuggle a letter out.[30]

Perceived as the weaker sex and marginalized in religious rituals, the women were under less pressure to conform to the image of the demonic Jew. In the trial records, they emerged as individuals, unlike many of the men whose personalities were submerged in the official story of ritual murder. We learn of the solidarity between Sara, Schönlein, and Anna. We sense Sara's fragility, we admire Schönlein's resourcefulness, and we feel Anna's youth and vulnerability.

Perhaps the sharpest contrast was between Anna and Gütlein. Daughter of a respectable family and wife of Israel the son of community leader Samuel, the twenty-three-year-old Anna was well educated. Fluent in Italian and German, she could also read Hebrew. On 9 March 1476, during an interrogation at Samuel's house, the podestà asked Anna to describe the liturgy of Passover, specifically the maledictions against the Egyptians. Anna replied she did not remember the exact Hebrew words but she could find the passage if she had the Haggadah, which was lying by her bed. When the book was brought, Anna could not turn the pages due to the pain of previous torture sessions but identified the passage when the pages were turned for her.[31]

In contrast, Gütlein, Engel's sister, a woman in her mid-thirties, came from a very different world. Ignorant of Hebrew, Gütlein was familiar with the world of popular magic. Interrogated about the powers of Christian blood, Gütlein told the podestà this story: there was a time in her past when master Jacob of Cracow instructed her and Süsslein in the magical arts from his book of spells. If they poured Christian blood into a well, stood over the water until they saw their own reflections, and uttered the lightning spell, it would storm and hail. For the benefit of the podestà, "she said those very words," the clerk recorded, "but the podestà did not want it written down, in order to avoid a greater evil."[32]

The tension between the household of the newcomer, Engel, and the other two Jewish families was also reflected in the testimony of Engel's sister, Gütlein. She gave the impression of toughness, a defensive trait, perhaps, due to her disappointments in life. As late as 11 March 1476, under torture, she tried to defend her brother's household. Asserting that nobody there was involved in the alleged murder, Gütlein shifted the blame to the other two households, confessing to the magistrates that her dead sister-in-law, Süsslein, had told her that the households of Samuel and Tobias had killed the boy.[33] Her fierce family loyalty, however, meant little in the face of authorities who were convinced of the guilt not of one or two families but of the entire Jewish people.

CHAPTER ELEVEN

JUDGMENT IN ROME

In a stern letter dated 3 April 1476, Pope Sixtus IV warned Bishop Hinderbach, "After the return of the venerable Brother Baptista, Bishop of Ventimiglia, whom we sent to you due to the trial of the Jews, with full knowledge that we have appointed a commission from my venerable brethren cardinals of the Holy Roman Church for this matter, from which commission a strong prohibition has been issued, we learn, nevertheless. . . . you are undertaking everyday new measures against the aforementioned Jews." Sixtus threatened suspension of his office, ordering Hinderbach to desist from "doing anything further against the Jews or their possessions, but to remove the women, and the others still living, from incarceration" to a comfortable and safe place.[1] Hinderbach complied. The cessation of the trial in Trent against the Jewish women signaled a dramatic turn: now, Hinderbach's conduct and the ritual murder trial itself came under investigation. The scene shifted to the curia; the cast changed to cardinals, humanists, and ambassadors; and the plot thickened with diplomatic maneuvers, bribery, innuendo, and committee deliberations. This drama concluded only in June 1478, two and a half years after the appointment of the commission of cardinals in Rome.

The pontificate of Sixtus IV transformed Rome. From a depopulated, desolate medieval commune, the Eternal City was becoming the glorious capital of Christendom, with splendid churches, public structures, and palaces. Much of the credit went to Sixtus. He proclaimed 1475 as the year of the Jubilee, restored churches, built a new bridge (named after himself) across the Tiber, and attracted numerous pilgrims to Rome. A patron of the arts and learning, Sixtus commissioned work on the chapel that would bear his name, established the Vatican Library, and encouraged humanists at the papal court. Finally, he expanded the college of cardinals, making thirty-four appointments in his lifetime (including six of his nephews), and established the papal curia as the major court in Europe.[2]

Many nationalities settled in Rome, clustered in neighborhoods or even entire quarters, with their own markets and places of worship. Dating back to the third century, the Jewish settlement, concentrated along the right bank of the Tiber, had a strong communal tradition, with its synagogues, hospital, schools, printing press, and judicial autonomy, recognized by papal and munici-

Figure 8. Letter from Sixtus IV to Johannes Hinderbach, dated 3 April 1476.
Reproduced courtesy of Archivio di Stato, Trent.

pal authorities. Notarial deeds for the period 1454–84 recorded the names of 402 Jews, most of them male. By comparison, the first census in Rome (1526–27) counted 373 families and 1,772 individuals in the Jewish community. The Jewish population in 1475 would probably have been close to the 1526 figure.[3] In contrast to most Jewish communities, where banking represented the most prominent occupation, in Rome the physicians were the eminent members of the community. Highly respected by Christians, Jewish physicians treated many Gentile clients, including members of the papal court.[4] Other occupations included a wide range of handicrafts and moneylending, although practiced on a small scale.

In Rome, Jews and Christians co-existed peacefully; they did business together, serving as witnesses and guarantors for each others' legal transactions. Even Jewish converts maintained contacts with friends and relatives in the Jewish community. Crucial to this tolerant milieu was the relationship between the Roman Jews and the papacy. In recognizing papal sovereignty, the Jews acknowledged their political dependence on the pope, whose secular powers were increasingly emphasized in the Renaissance. In 1459, the papacy instituted the first Jewish tax, collected in 1472, with partial success, under the pontificate of Sixtus IV.[5] In addition to their fiscal contributions to the papal state, Roman Jews participated in papal elections through a rite of homage. After the election by the cardinals in conclave, during the papal procession from St. Peter's to the church of St. John Lateran, leaders of the Jewish community met the papal train at Monte Giordano and offered the Torah to the pope, asking for his approval. The new pope, holding the Torah, commended the law but condemned its interpretation by the Jews and dropped the Torah to the ground, in accordance with ritual.[6]

When news of the Trent ritual murder trial reached Rome, the Jewish community appealed for papal intervention. After the return of the apostolic commissioner, leaders of the community continued to petition the papal curia, sometimes with large monetary gifts. They were, however, strangers to the Vatican palace, unfamiliar with its corridors of power.

Politics at the papal curia revolved around two axes: one, represented by the Sacred College of Cardinals, constituted an oligarchy, the highest collective of ecclesiastical dignitaries, from whose ranks the pope was elected; the other, institutionalized favoritism, was the inner entourage of the pope, which consisted principally of his nephews. The two axes intersected in the person of Sixtus IV, who brought many nephews to the curia during his pontificate, elevating six to the cardinalate. Many forces propelled the rotation of these axes—intervention by foreign monarchs, the interest of national churches, and the ambition of the leading Italian noble families. The unprecedented concentration of wealth and power in the papacy created a brilliant culture; its artistic, humanist, and architectural representations glorified the restoration of Rome, in both its spiritual and secular dimensions.

Hinderbach knew this world. As imperial ambassador to the papacy, a friend of Pius II, and a collector of humanist manuscripts, Hinderbach had many contacts in the curia.[7] Although the investigation in Rome continued for some two and a half years, Hinderbach's persistence and his knowledge of curial politics eventually paid off.

At the end of 1475, Sixtus IV appointed a special congregation of six cardinals to continue the work of the apostolic commission. In addition to two Venetian patricians, cardinals Marco Barbo and Giovanni Michiel (nephews of the previous pope, Paul II), Francesco Gonzaga, the cardinal of Arezzo, Tirasonense, and Ravenna also served. A younger son of the duke of Mantua, Gonzaga represented the new type of cardinal, appointed to serve the political interests of the leading Italian noble families. Among his many benefices was a canonate in the cathedral of Trent. Perhaps the most distinguished member of the commission was Cardinal Barbo, bishop of Vicenza, known for his austerity and piety, a jurist by training, and a major humanist and patron of learning in Rome.[8]

As soon as he found out about the appointment of the special congregation, Hinderbach dispatched two ambassadors to Rome. On their arrival, the two jurists—Wilhelm Rottaler (Hinderbach's secretary) and Approvinus de Approvinis—paid court to Cristoforo della Rovere, archbishop of Tarantas and nephew of the pope, who welcomed the Trentini and promised to help end the investigation. Through his ambassadors, Hinderbach received a steady stream of news and gossip: how Dei Giudici had fallen out of favor with Sixtus; how Cardinal Barbo was sympathetic to the Jews; and how the Jews left no stone unturned in their efforts against Hinderbach.[9]

Forewarned, Hinderbach was able to mobilize his forces. He wrote to Cardinal Barbo on 22 February, denying the charge that he had confiscated the goods belonging to the Jews, except for some books for the episcopal library; he protested that the investigation impinged upon his secular jurisdiction; he denounced the bishop of Ventimiglia as a friend of Jews who had promised them freedom; and he ended by pleading for the cause of Simon.[10] Consistent with his tactics against the apostolic commissioner, Hinderbach focused on Simon's martyrdom and miracles, not on the conduct of the trial. At the end of August 1476 he sent documentation of the miracles attributed to Little Simon to the commission of cardinals.[11]

Unrelentingly, Hinderbach argued his case. Many supported him. According to his correspondence, the Franciscans in Venice and Vicenza emerged as strong allies. In Vicenza, Father Nicolaus preached his Lenten sermon on Simon's martyrdom. In Venice, Father Michael de Milano tirelessly propagated Simon's cause from the pulpit; he congratulated the bishop on the many miracles attributed to Simon; in turn, Hinderbach sent the friars relics of Simon; and the Franciscans promised to exercise their influence among the Venetian patriciate and in Rome.[12] Among the secular clergy, Bishop Heinrich of Regensburg and Bishop Angelo of Feltre declared their support; Heinrich wrote to Hinderbach on 15 October 1476 as his "most honorable friend" and sent his chaplain, Gregorius Griespeck, to plead Hinderbach's case in Rome.[13]

And then, there were the Jewish women. In January 1477, the Trentini triumphantly announced the baptism of three Jewish women and one man. After the cessation of the trial in early April 1476, the Jewish women disappeared from the official records until their baptisms in January 1477. Still under house arrest, separated from their children, who had been released in November 1475 by order of the commissioner, the women were pawns of the prince-bishop. Did their silence mean that their spirits were broken? Only survival mattered. They could not have resisted the combination of coercion and persuasion; perhaps they thought baptism would save their lives.

On 13 January 1477, "after the singing of solemn vespers," Schönlein, Anna, Sara, and Salomon (Tobias' cook) appeared before the episcopal chapel, the Chapel of St. Andrea, in the Buonconsiglio.[14] A crowd was gathered: Doctor Alexandro de Madus de Bassano acted as the papal legate; Ambrosius Staspel, Udulric Lichtensteiner, and Konrad Hinderbach (the bishop's brother) represented the cathedral canons; lords Paulo and Georgio, sons of the doctor of law, Antonio de Terlaco in addition to noblemen and servants of the episcopal court and, of course, Hinderbach himself were present. After they approached the altar, the women "humbly asked for baptism," in the words of the notary, "and prayed to the lord, the Virgin Mary, the angels, the apostles, and the saints." Hinderbach asked them whether they desired baptism "voluntarily, without any other reaction, violence, fear, terror and suggestion, but only on account of divine inspiration and their own will . . . and conscience, without any dissimulation of sorrow or fraud, but to preserve in the Catholic faith until the end of their lives, with firmness and sincerity." At this signal, well rehearsed beforehand, the three women responded "yes," clearly, in German. Hinderbach granted their request. He then asked the women whether they acknowledged the crimes of their husbands, sons, and servants, "who tortured and spilled the blood of the innocent Simon out of hatred in order to abuse Christian blood, thus blaspheming against God, etc. as contained in the trial and inquisition records." After the expected affirmative reply, Hinderbach asked whether the women were truly sorry for the crimes their men had committed. After this dialogue of contrition and submission, the bishop warned them against "Jewish perfidy" and physical and spiritual death, should they relapse in faith. Then, Hinderbach performed the rite of exorcism, first on Sara, then the other two. Next came the prayers and finally baptism: Sara became Clara; Schönlein, Elizabeth; and Anna, Susanna. Salomon was baptized by Konrad Hinderbach; he became Giovanni.

A more humiliating scene followed on January 26. At noon, the four converts donned white robes and were led to St. Peter's, where they beheld the wounds of Little Simon and prayed for his intercession.[15] The trial had destroyed their lives; baptismal water washed away their identities. In their new incarnations, the women lived out lives of apparitions, forever lost to historical record and memory.

Hinderbach did not waste time. By mid-February 1477, his ambassador, Wilhelm Rottaler, had already presented the documents of the baptisms of Sara, Schönlein, Anna, and Salomon to Cardinal Barbo.[16] The conversions made an impression. Hinderbach's partisans included men influential in various institutions of the curia; three of them are prominently named in the correspondence and other sources: Cristoforo della Rovere, Bartolomeo dei Sacchi, better known as Platina, and Giovanni Francesco de Pavini.

A nephew of the pope, Cristoforo della Rovere was not as famous as Giuliano, the future Pope Julius II. Nonetheless, his presence at the Vatican reflected the transformation of the curia into a more openly secular court, where political power flowed through personal connections. He was one of the first visited by Hinderbach's ambassadors. As castellan of Sant'Angelo, responsible for the defense of the Vatican, Cristoforo held one of the most important offices in the curia. In March 1477, Sixtus nominated five men to the Sacred College, among them his nephews, Cristoforo and Girolamo Basso della Rovere. On 10 December, both men, together with another nephew, were raised to the purple.[17] Quick to offer congratulations, Hinderbach expressed his own gratitude for the cardinal's support.[18] As a powerful man, Cristoforo's opinions were heeded, not least for the fact that he had the ear of the pope.

A member of the Roman Academy and leading humanist, Platina represented another segment of the curia. The author of a papal biography, *Liber de vita Christi ac omnium pontificum,* commissioned by Sixtus IV, Platina enjoyed the patronage of the pope, to whom he dedicated the manuscript in 1475. In the same year, Sixtus IV appointed Platina the head of the newly created Vatican Library, an event immortalized by the fresco painting of Melozzo da Forli.[19] In his "Invective," Dei Giudici called Platina a friend of Hinderbach, who pleaded the prince-bishop's case with the cardinals without much knowledge of the affair.[20] In any event, Platina's help was significant enough to merit singular mention in a report by Approvinus to Hinderbach, dated 20 April 1478.[21]

The third man, Giovanni Francesco de Pavini, was a jurist at the curia. A theologian and a canon lawyer, Pavini was summoned to serve on the Tribunal of the Rota by Pius II, after many years of teaching at Padua. As one of the three auditors of the Rota assisting the commission of cardinals, Pavini wrote two legal briefs on the ritual murder trial, which were published after the conclusion of the investigation with financial backing from Hinderbach.[22] The first brief argued for the unexceptionability of the trial against the Jews in Trent. Its arguments, based on the theologic-canonical doctrine of "Jewish servitude," denied full legal capacity to Jews on account of the legal principle of bad reputation (*mala fama*). The second brief invalidated the testimony of Anzelino Austoch and annulled the work of the apostolic commissioner. . Furthermore, Pavini accused Dei Giudici of exceeding his mandate by staging another trial instead of observing events in Trent, of acting clandestinely in favor of the Jews, and, by freeing the Jewish children, of damning their souls because they were not baptized along with their mothers. "Since Jews are serfs," Pavini declared, Christian princes could baptize their children without parental consent.[23]

Hinderbach's position before the commission of cardinals emphasized three points. First, the prince-bishop argued for the truth of the ritual murder and hence, the propriety of the trial against the Jews. Second, he protested the intervention in his exercise of temporal jurisdiction as a secular prince. Finally, and most importantly, Hinderbach hoped to present Little Simon for canonization.

Dei Giudici, the bishop of Ventimiglia, seemed to be carrying on a lonely fight. In his "Apologia" to the commission of cardinals, Dei Giudici forcefully stated his objections to Trent:

> Finally, may your lordships diligently consider the peril which would be incumbent on the Christian religion, on account of the dealings in Trent, and the lies that would reach the ignorant, the unlearned, and the simple folk. For just as it is known that true miracles are frequently effected by God for the confirmation of faith, so the holy doctors of the Church are certain that false and simulated miracles, concocted out of human devices and cleverness, would lead to the destruction of the same faith. It is evident from the Holy Scriptures that the Antichrist performs false miracles, not real ones: because there are no arms more strong, no arguments more forceful, no beguiling lies more pernicious, for the destruction of the Faith, than the fraudulent inventions of such false miracles. They even call into doubt the miracles of the apostles, martyrs, and saints of old, which were, however, splendid and true miracles, not false ones.[24]

Attacked by Hinderbach's partisans as a "Jew lover" and "agent of the Antichrist," Dei Giudici struck back with ferocity. In a private letter to Platina, Dei Giudici related the temerity of the Trentini in comparing Little Simon to Christ. "When I was presiding over the tribunal in Rovereto," he wrote, "the procurator of the Trentini dared to protest, not in a secluded place, but in front of a multitude, that he and the Trentini adore his blessed one just like Christ, to use his words, and just like the Messiah: they preferred him, as he said, to all the virgins, martyrs, apostles, and all the saints of the holy Church of God." In the letter, Dei Giudici asked Platina: "Can you defend this, which the human ear abhors, without your highest vituperation?"[25]

The cardinals faced a difficult case. Skeptical of unconfirmed reports of miracles, the late medieval Church was scrupulous in decisions involving the conferring of sanctity on local and popular *beati*. In particular, the Holy See consistently refused to recognize the victims of alleged ritual murders, whose cults were popular in England, France, and Germany.[26] Condemning the trial, however, would cause a great scandal: Hinderbach was an important prince-bishop with powerful connections; the territory of Trent belonged to the Empire, and Archduke Sigismund had expressed his approval of the trial; the cult of Little Simon was rapidly gaining popularity, not only in Trent, but also in neighboring Veneto and Lombardy; and the Franciscans, the pope's own order, were staunch supporters.

Like any committee at work, the commission of cardinals took time with the laborious task of the gathering of testimonies, the examination of documents, and the lengthy deliberations. Personnel changes further slowed down the pace of work.[27] In February 1477, Cardinal Giacomo Ammannati Piccolomini replaced the cardinal of Ravenna, whose death was preceded by a long period of ill health.[28] In fact, nine cardinals died during the 1470s and were replaced by worldly men appointed for political considerations.[29] Moreover, there were the usual administrative delays, when other matters preoccupied the pontiff and the Sacred College. At the end of January 1478, in a letter to Hinderbach, Approvinus wrote of the conclusion of the deliberations and his confidence in the outcome.[30] Then, Sixtus fell ill and the issuance of the papal bull was delayed. In March Dei Giudici argued for the interrogation of the Jewish women in Rome, a request that was denied.[31] Rumors circulated through the city. One story, originating in the Jewish communities of Rovereto and Rome, reported the capture of Trent and Hinderbach by Habsburg troops and sent Hinderbach's ambassador into a momentary panic.[32] Another rumor in mid-April filled Rome with the story of host desecration and the burnings of Jews in Bavaria.[33] For the remainder of the spring, Sixtus tried to avert war between Rome and Florence in the aftermath of the Pazzi Conspiracy. This conspiracy, a failed attempt to assassinate Lorenzo de' Medici and institute a propapal regime, was an outrageous scheme encouraged by Girolamo Riario, a nephew of the pope.

In the end, Pavini's legal opinions laid the foundation for the cardinal's report. On 20 June 1478, the papal bull was published. Sixtus IV cleared Hinderbach of all suspicions; the commission of cardinals, who had diligently examined all pertinent records, concluded that the trial was conducted in conformity with legal procedure. Sixtus praised the bishop's zeal but admonished Hinderbach, on his conscience, not to permit anything contrary to the 1247 Decretum of Innocent IV (which prohibited ritual murder trials) in promoting devotion to Simon nor to disobey the Holy See or canonical prescriptions. Moreover, Sixtus forbade any Christian, on this or any other occasion, without papal judgment, to kill or mutilate Jews, or extort money from them, or to prevent them from practicing their rites as permitted by law. He concluded by asking Hinderbach to reunite the children with their baptized mothers and to restore the confiscated dowries to the women.[34]

Hinderbach's partisans hailed the papal bull. The judgment, however, was hardly a vindication. Although Sixtus IV exonerated Hinderbach, he condemned ritual murder trials not only in reference to the Decretum of Innocent IV but in vigorous language prohibiting violence against the Jews.

Still, the outcome represented a victory for Trent. The cult of Little Simon grew in popularity, propagated by the tireless effort of Hinderbach and the Franciscans. Long engaged in anti-Jewish polemic, the order of Minor friars had been preaching the prohibition of Jewish moneylending and the establishment of Christian banks for the poor, the *Monte di Pietà*.[35] Simon became a new cause. A favorite theme in Franciscan preaching, especially in Lenten sermons, the death of Little Simon was also depicted in frescoes; iconography often represented the "martyrdom" in the context of the Passion of Christ, with "St. Simon triumphant" in the pose of the Child Jesus or in the company of the Virgin Mary. Almost all frescoes and iconographic representations of Simon in northern Italy were found in churches of the Franciscan-Observants.[36]

The good will of the pope could not prevent anti-Semitic violence. In 1478, ritual murder accusations were raised against the Jews of Reggio and Mantua; in 1479, in Arena, near Milan, a trial was conducted; in 1480, several Jews living at Portobuffuolà near Treviso were executed on the charge of child kidnapping; the same year, a similar accusation was heard in Verona.[37] The chain of anti-Jewish events was manifest in Vicenza: from the report of the alleged murder of Simon in 1475, to the Lenten sermons of

Figure 9. The Martyrdom of Simon of Trent. Tempera on panel by Gandolfino di Roreto d'Asti. Piedmont, late fifteenth century. Reproduced courtesy of the Israel Museum, Jerusalem.

the Franciscan Nicholas in 1476, leading to the termination of all contracts with Jewish moneylenders in 1479, concluding with the expulsion of all Jews in 1486 and the establishment of the Monte di Pietà.[38]

If the Franciscans helped to excite devotion to the "Little Martyr" in northern Italy, the position of Trent in the Holy Roman Empire spread Little Simon's cult to Austria and southern Germany. Not surprisingly, the Tirol, a region plagued by legends of blood accusations, produced paintings and other iconographic depictions of Simon.[39] The trial in Trent activated local legends about child murders: the story of the alleged 1442 ritual murder in Lienz was first written down in September 1475; and in Rinn, the boy Andreas Oxner, found murdered in 1462, was posthumously honored as a victim of the Jews.[40] Simon's story also affected the Innsbruck court. In spite of his initial opposition, Archduke Sigismund approved of the trial, as Hinderbach reported.[41] Sigismund's successor in Innsbruck, Maximilian, his nephew and son of Emperor Friedrich III, was a strong supporter of the cult: as a young prince, he first showed interest as early as 1479;[42] as archduke, he erected a silver monument in Simon's honor, with an inscription in gold at the base to commemorate the building;[43] in 1495, he ordered the provost of St. Peter's in Trent to open Simon's coffin for the pious to view;[44] and when Maximilian was proclaimed emperor in 1508, the relics of Simon were displayed in a procession in his honor.[45] Through books, chronicles, and folk songs, the story of Simon's "martyrdom" reached a wide area in central and southern Germany.[46]

A distinct counterpoint to the chorus of Christian glorification, Jewish voices commemorated Trent in sorrow and anger. The earliest testimony was the *Kinah,* or the "Lamentations of Trent," composed by Rabbi Solomon Levi of Verona, a family friend to Samuel, Brünnlein, and Israel.[47] "Hills of Trent, may you not have rain or dew / Seven times may you fall and not rise," thus the verses of the *Kinah,* echoing Biblical verses (II Samuel 1:21 and

Amos 5:2) and the rabbinic injunction against the city and its territory, the *herem,* or "separation."[48] The Lamentations, probably composed during the second half of 1475, mentioned only Samuel and Israel, who went to their deaths courageously, in testimony of their faith. A later source, the *Emek Habacha* of Rabbi Joseph ben Joshua ha Cohen (1495–1575), a Sephardic Jew, contained a longer entry. Written between 1558 and 1563, *Emek Habacha* was a chronicle of the sufferings of the Jews. Under the entry "5235, 15 Nisan," Rabbi Joseph recounted the story of Trent in considerable detail: he identified Anzelino (Enzo in his version) as the child killer, who planted the body in Samuel's house; he praised "Moscheh" (Old Moses), who died without confessing; he mentioned the alleged miracles, the visit of the apostolic commissioner, popular violence against him, and the investigation in Rome. In this account, Hinderbach was the chief villain, who staged the trial to rob the Jews of their possessions. Rabbi Joseph took comfort in the refusal of the papacy, "up to this day," to elevate Simon from *beatus* to *sanctus.* He then invoked the Lord "to lift the veil of blindness from the eyes of the people, who are of uncircumcised hearts and believe in such untruths."[49]

His cause defeated in the curia, Dei Giudici left the clamor in Rome to become the governor of Benevento. After serving as papal legate in France during 1480, he returned in good grace to the papal court. Promised the archbishopric of Patrasso in 1484, Dei Giudici died on 15 April of the same year in Rome, before he could assume the new office.[50]

Sixtus died a few months later, on 12 August, leaving behind a city filled with monuments to his memory.

Hinderbach, obsessed with the project of Simon's canonization, did not live to see his little martyr elevated to sainthood. He died in Trent on 21 September 1486.

After his tenure as podestà in Trent ended, Giovanni de Salis returned to his native Brescia. He served as a legal consultant in the 1480 Portobuffolà ritual murder trial, in which four Jews were condemned to death.[51] In 1493 he met the Franciscan Bernardino da Feltre, who went on preaching against Jewish moneylenders.[52]

There is no record of the fate of Salomon, Sara, Schönlein, Anna, and Gütlein, nor of their children.

EPILOGUE

"Little Simon" lived on for a long time. In Trent, a chapel in St. Peter's was dedicated to his "martyrdom." Vigorously promoted by Observant Franciscans and humanists, his cult spread to many communities in northern Italy and southern Germany.[1] During the general Church Council (1545–1563) that defined the doctrines and character of the Counter-Reformation, Little Simon attracted many visiting ecclesiastical dignitaries. In 1588, Pope Sixtus V conferred official sanction on the local cult. Into the seventeenth century, poems, hagiographies, paintings, and other iconographic representations celebrated the death of the innocent child.

Defenders of the cult emerged when skeptics criticized the official story of ritual murder. The German Protestant Christof Wagenseil (1633–1705) published a treatise in which he questioned the reality of alleged ritual murders in the past.[2] In 1747, the Franciscan Benedetto Bonelli (1704–1783) published the first serious study based on the trial records; the *Dissertazione apologetica sul martirio del Beato Simone da Trento,* as its title suggests, was a defense of the cult, aimed at refuting the thesis of Wagenseil point for point and presented his work in the tradition of hagiography.

The next full-scale defense of the cult, the two-volume *Storia del Beato Simone da Trento,* published in 1902, also came from the pen of a Trent clergyman, the canon Giuseppe Divina. Again, the challenge came from the north, from Hermann Strack, a Protestant professor of evangelical theology in Berlin, and from the German-Jewish historian Moritz Stern, who had published books critical of ritual murder trials, in 1892 and 1893, respectively. Alarmed by a new wave of ritual murder accusations sweeping central and eastern Europe, Strack published an impassioned work to expose the folly of anti-Semitism and superstitions about Jewish ritual use of Christian blood.[3] Stern, who had collected and published papal bulls condemning ritual murder trials, visited Trent, an occasion remembered with suspicion by Divina.[4] In the face of this joint Protestant-Jewish German assault on Italian Catholicism, Divina judged that it was not enough that the Vatican publication, *La Civiltà Cattolica,* had published excerpts of the 1475 trial interrogations deposited in the Vatican Archives.[5] Divina read almost every single document related to the trial then available in Trent. His book repeated, in essence, the official story, filled the gaps in the documentation with his vivid imagination and rendered a coherent, massive, and seamless narrative, thereby creating a new anti-Jewish incident to add to the history of ritual murder.

If these apologists of the Church repeated the official history in defense of the trial, their accounts never went unchallenged. Josef Scherer, in his legal history of Jews in Austrian lands, *Die Rechtsverhältnisse der Juden in den deutsch-österreichischen Ländern,* published in Leipzig in 1901, examined some of the trial records in Innsbruck (the former archive of the prince-bishops was transferred from Trent to Innsbruck and back to Trent in 1919), demon-

Figure 10. Simon as "the little martyr" and saint. Baroque bas-reliefs, façade, Palazzo Salvadori, Trent. Note the covering of the penis, a modification of the original iconography to accommodate Baroque sensibilities. Reproduced courtesy of Provincia Autonoma di Trento, Museo provinciale d'arte.

strated the impossibility of the charge, and accused the Trentini of having conducted an illegal trial in 1475. In 1903, Giuseppe Menestrina published an influential article, significantly entitled "The Jews of Trent," and not "Simon of Trent," a critical historical analysis in the spirit of liberal anticlericalism, in which Bernardino de Feltre and popular Catholic superstitions appeared as the evil forces.[6]

The events of the twentieth century transformed the discourse in accounts of the Trent trial. The Holocaust, the German occupation of Italy, and the Second World War constructed a radically different context for the telling of a Counter-Story. Critical voices were heard, inside and outside the Catholic Church. In 1963, Gemma Volli attacked the cult, blaming Franciscan preaching and the German immigrants in Trent for anti-Semitism;[7] in 1964, the German Dominican Willehad Paul Eckert, after studying the trial records, published a historical study refuting the cult.[8] Finally, in 1965, after the Second Vatican Council, the cult was abolished by papal decree.[9] More recently, the old official story, self-righteous and emotional, gave way to a sentimental but uncritical counter-story.[10]

If the record of the ritual murder trial still contains different voices from the past, monuments to the death of Little Simon have lost their original signification. Once, the spirit of the martyred boy pervaded the buildings and monuments to his memory. Then, after 1965, his remains were removed from St. Peter's and laid to rest. Today, a visitor to Trent can walk up the Via Manci from the State Archive and, within a few minutes, stand before the Palazzo Salvadori, on the site of Samuel's house in 1475, and the scene of the alleged slaughter. On the façade of the Baroque palace are two bas-reliefs depicting the death and ascension of Simon. For centuries, these images without words told the official stories of Simon, Samuel, Tobias, Engel, and the Jews of Trent. Today, they have lost the power of enchantment and have turned back to stone.

APPENDIX:
A NOTE ON SOURCES

Eleven complete or partial texts of the trial records have survived, including the Yeshiva manuscript. Nine are written in Latin, two in German. Anna Esposito and Diego Quaglioni give a full description of six of the Latin manuscripts in *Processi* 1: 97–102; the discussion of those texts here is intended to supplement their critical notes. After a brief description of the manuscripts, I shall address several questions of textuality raised by Esposito and Quaglioni, particularly regarding their postulation of an Ur-text of the trial proceedings. Finally, I shall discuss the textual and linguistic differences between the German and Latin scripts.

The eleven manuscripts are as follows:

1. *Vatican City,* Archivio Segreto Vaticano, Arch. Castel S. Angelo, n. 6495. This Latin manuscript was the one sent by Bishop Hinderbach to the commission of cardinals on 15 November 1475. It does not include the interrogations of Moses of Bamberg, Isaac son of Jacob, Lazarus of Seravalle, Moses the

schoolmaster (Young Moses), Joaff, Israel the painter, Sara, Anna, Gütlein, and Schönlein. This manuscript serves as the basic text for the published critical edition, *Processi contro gli ebrei di Trento (Processi)*, edited by Anna Esposito and Diego Quaglioni.

2. *Vienna,* ÖNB, Cod. Lat. 5360. All of the interrogations are included in this Latin manuscript, except those of Roper the tailor. This manuscript was first sent to Emperor Friedrich III and passed on to the city of Vienna; on the leather binding are the words "Ex bibliotheca civica vindobonensi."

3. *Trent,* Museo Diocesano, Cod. S. Pietro. This Latin manuscript served as the main source for Giuseppe Divina's *Storia del beato Simone da Trento, compilata sui processi autentici istituiti contro gli Ebrei e sopra altri documenti contemporanei.* (2 vols.; Trent, 1902).

4. *Trent,* Archivio di Stato (AST), Archivio Principesco-Vescovile (APV), Sezione Latina (SL), Capsa 69 (C), n. 1b. Inscribed "Processus contra iudeos habitus Tridenti anno domini 1475," this Latin manuscript consists of the testimonies of the Christian witnesses and physicians; the interrogations of the two Seligmans, and of Israel son of Samuel, Vital, Samuel, Engel, Tobias, Old Moses, and Mayer; and finally, the testimonies of the Schweizer, Dorothea, and Roper the tailor.

5. *Trent,* AST, APV, SL, C. 69, n. 1c. Identical to AST, APV, SL, C. 69, n. 1b. The 140 folios of this Latin manuscript are copied in three hands in notarial script.

6. *Trent,* AST, APV, SL, C. 69, n. 2. Inscribed "In causa Beati Simonis," this Latin manuscript is similar in handwriting and binding to AST, APV, SL, C. 69, n. 1b. It consists of the interrogations of Joaff, Isaac, Young Moses, Lazarus, and Moses son of Aaron.

7. *Trent,* AST, APV, SL, C. 69, n. 3. This Latin manuscript, inscribed "Processus inquisitionis contra Israehelem Hebreum filium Mohar hebrei de Brandenburg," consists only of the interrogations of Israel the painter (the convert Wolfgang).

8. *Trent,* AST, APV, SL, C. 69, n. 4 (I). Inscribed "Processus inquisitionis contra Sarram," this Latin manuscript contains the interrogations of Sara, Schönlein, Gütlein, and Anna.

9. *Trent,* AST, APV, SL, C. 69, n. 4 (II). This Latin manuscript consists of unbound folio pages numbered 89 to 210. It is written in one hand, in black ink, without the headings in red ink of the other manuscripts. It consists of the interrogations of the two Seligmans, Israel, Vital, Samuel, and Mayr, as well as those of the Schweizer and Roper.

10. *Trent,* AST, APV, SL, C. 69, n. 1a. This German manuscript, with the inscription "Liber miraculorum beati Symonis Martyri Tridentii" on the binding, is almost identical in content to the YM. It is written in black ink, with red ink for title headings. Two hands can be identified, a smaller notarial hand replacing the first chancerial hand on folio 324v. Unlike the YM, it is not illuminated and the line spaces reserved for the Hebrew Haggadah excerpts are left blank.

11. *New York,* Yeshiva University Library, 1478 German manuscript, 614 folios, 12.24 × 8.5 inches (310 × 215 mm). The text bears the inscription "Prozess gegen die Juden von Trient." This German manuscript dates after 20 June 1478, the date of the papal bull confirming the findings of the commission of cardinals, which, in the German translation, opens the manuscript. It includes most of the initial testimonies of the Christian witnesses and all the interrogations of the Jewish men and women, including quotations in Hebrew, given both in the original and with Latin transliterations. Excluded are the testimonies of the Schweizer, Dorothea, and Roper.

Clearly, there are numerous historical and textual problems presented by the extant manuscripts of the trial. In preparing the Vatican manuscript for publication, Anna Esposito and Diego Quaglioni produced an excellent critical edition of the Latin text that includes variant readings from the other Latin manuscripts. However, they have not consulted the German scripts, which help solve certain textual problems but present new ones as well.

Variations in spellings, especially regarding personal and place names—a reflection of the multiple translations between German, Italian, and Latin—present an irritating but by no means intractable problem. In the German texts, for example, some of the Jews are referred to by their German names, not by their Italianized or Latinized names: thus, Seligman instead of Bonaventure, Mayer instead of Mohar, Engel instead of Angelo, Schönlein and Gütlein instead of Bella and Bona. As may be expected, the YM is more reliable in German orthography than is the *Processi*. For example, when the night watchman Antoniolo testified that he heard voices in Samuel's house telling the crying boy to keep quiet; his words are recorded in the *Processi* (doc. 10, p. 122) as "sbaich pub." In the YM (fol. 16) the words are "sweig pub." German place names are recorded idiosyncratically in the Latin texts: hence, "Sbircemborg" is really Würzburg, "Hol de Saxonia" is Halle, and so on.

Other inconsistencies between the *Processi* and the YM are more difficult to reconcile. Differing dates are recorded for two interrogations. According to the YM (fol. 93), the "Other Seligman" (al. Bonaventure), was interrogated on 27 March 1475; the *Processi* (p. 153) lists that interrogation as taking place on 28 March 1475. Again, according to the YM (fols. 147–49), Engel was interrogated twice on 31 March 1475; the *Processi* (pp. 281–83) lists the two interrogations as occurring on consecutive days, 30 and 31 March. One can attribute these minor variations to careless or overworked scribes, but other inconsistencies, albeit they are few, are harder to explain. For example, the YM (fol. 10) refers to Engel's father as Samuel of Bern, but the *Processi* (p. 114) refers to him as Salomon of Verona.

Perhaps one might resolve these textual problems by reconstructing a first text of the trial proceedings, as Esposito and Quaglioni suggest. The idea of an "Ur-text," however, attractive as it may be, does not address the problem of authenticity; the historian still faces multiple problems of translation—from the spoken word to the written transcript, from Italian and German into Latin, and above all, from the words spoken, no longer heard, into an experience with a tragic past.

NOTES

INTRODUCTION

1. The following is based on R. Po-chia Hsia, "Il manoscritto di Yeshiva sul processo contro gli ebrei di Trento," in Rogger. The Yeshiva Manuscript was first sold in 1937 at an auction at Sotheby's in London to Lessing J. Rosenwald, who presented it to the American Jewish Historical Society at Waltham, Mass., on the condition that it be sealed for fifty years. See "An Unusual Purchase at Sotheby's," in *Recollections of A Collector by Lessing J. Rosenwald* (Jenkintown, Pa., 1976), 29–33. I am indebted to Professor G. N. Knauer of Philadelphia for this reference.

2. On the library of the Württemberg dukes, see Volker Press, "Herzog Ulrich (1498–1550)," in *900 Jahre Haus Württemberg. Leben und Leistung für Land und Volk,* ed. Robert Uhland (Stuttgart, 1985), pp. 110–35.

3. The mandate of expulsion, dated 9 October 1477, is published in A. L. Reyscher, ed., *Vollständige historische und kritisch bearbeitete Sammlung der württembergischen Gesetze,* vol. 11 (1841), pp. 14ff. Count Eberhard's testament is published in Reyscher, ed., *Vollständige historische Sammlung der württembergischen Gesetze,* vol. 2 (1829), p. 9.

4. This information was kindly communicated to me by Nikolaus Vielmetti of the Institut für Judaistik, Vienna.

5. YM, fol. 1 (in red ink): "Hye hebt sich nun von erst an die pabstlich Bull darinne unser heilig vater der pabst lobt den fleiß vnd allen gerichts handel der nachgeschribn proceß wider die Juden zu Trennt von des saligen unschuldigen kindleins genant Simon mit Recht vnd urtail volfürt, erkennt vnnd erklärt, das sollich proceß wider dieselbn Juden rechtlich vnd redlich gangen sey, als man hienach vernemen mag."

6. YM, fol. 4: "Nun hebent sich an hie all vnd yed obgemelt gerichts handl vnd proceß, wie die wider dy gottschenter vnd uneërer des leidens Jhesu Cristi die Juden zu Trennt von wegen des unschuldigen kindleins vnd saligen marters Simon, durch dieselben Juden jämerlich vnd unmenschlich gepeinigt vnd daselbn ermordt mit götlichem recht vnd urtail volfürt vnd gangen sein, vnd von erst von deselben kindleins verlust klag anpringen vnd suechen vnd vorraus von den großen mercklichen ware zaichen vnd anzaigen auff die bemelten Juden in menigerlay weis, als sich hin nach vinden wirt."

7. YM, fol. 23: "Als aber nun die Juden auff solliche vorgeschribne merckliche ware zaichen vnd anzaigen von des saligen kindleins wunten, vnd todt, nichts zewissen noch gleich zusagen wolten, haysthet die gerechtigkait vnd so großer handel, die warhait durch gerichts zwanng vnd ordnung gruntlich zuervorschen, da mit so groß ubel nicht ungestrafft, vnd nyemant unschuldiger fur was darub angevallen oder verdacht wurd. Darub dann der potestat daselbs ze Triennt schueff die benanten Juden, als er von ambts wegen schuldig was, weyt furzenemen vnd mit gerichts ordnung, wie sich zu sollichen sachen gepuret, erentstlich zefragen, wie wol aber in denselben gichtigungen oder fragen, in den nachgeschribnen processen von erst Bonaventur wällisch oder Saligman Jud in teutsch genant Samuel Juden Koch, vnd nach dem der ander Saligman, des Mayrs Juden sun, zu dem dritten Israhel Samuels sun, zu dem vierden Vital Samuels diener vnd erst zu dem fünfften Samuel selbs, mit seiner frag vnd bekantnuß geschriben stett, so hab ich doch mit demselben Samuel angefangen, vnd seine process von erst furgenomen, angesehen, das er vast der vordrist vnd mercklich ist, vnd der sachen der maist anweiser vnd ursacher gewesen ist, vnd nach meinem beduncken ettliche ding ordenlicher in seine bekanntnuß vnd aigenlicher gemelt vnd gesagt hat." The sequence referred to in the quotation ("as recorded in the following trials") is the one found in the Latin manuscripts.

8. In the text, Hans von Fundo is named as scribe of the interrogations; see YM, fols. 387, 389, 486. For Peter Rauter, see YM, fol. 486. See AST, APV, SL, C. 69, no. 35.

9. YM, fols. 474–75, 525.

10. The identity of the translator of the Yeshiva Manuscript has been brought to my attention by Professor G. N. Knauer of Philadelphia as this book goes to press. In 1938 Bernhard Bischoff suggested that the Dominican Erhardus

Streitperger from the Convent at Pettau, a student of the Christian Hebraist and anti-Jewish polemicist Peter Schwarz (Nigri), had translated the Latin trial records into German (See Bernhard Bischoff, "Frater Erhardus O.P., ein Hebrait des XV. Jahrhunderts," in *Historisches Jehrbuch* 58 (1938): 615–18; repr. in *Mittelalterliche Studien Ausgewählte Aufsätze zur Schriftkunde und Literaturgeschichte*, vol. 2, Stuttgart, 1967, 187–91). This argument is repeated by Thomas Kaeppeli in his *Scriptores Ordinis Praedicatorum Medii Aevi*, vol. 1, Rome, 1970, 373–74, and by Bischoff himself in *Die deutsche Literatur des Mittelalters, Verfasserlexikon*, vol. 2, Berlin, 1980, cc. 582–83. Erhard Streitperger was active in Regensburg around 1475 and could have worked from the Regensburg copy of the trial transcript that Bishop Heinrich brought back with him from Trent. Professor Knauer, however, advances the argument that the Erhard confessor identified with the translator of the German text was not Erhard Streitperger but another Dominican, Erhard von Pappenheim, friend of Johannes Reuchlin and confessor in Altenhohenau, a Dominican convent on the River Inn in the vicinity of Innsbruck. Given the proximity of Tirol to Trent and the role played by the German Dominicans in the affair, Knauer's argument seems just as plausible as Bischoff's.

CHAPTER ONE: THE PRINCE-BISHOP

1. On the relationship between documentary authority and narrative techniques in legal documents see Natalie Z. Davis, *Fiction in the Archives: Pardon Tales and Their Tellers in Sixteenth Century France* (Stanford, 1987).

2. The chief proponent of the view that stresses the continuity of anti-Semitism in European history is Léon Poliakov; see his *History of Anti-Semitism*, 4 vols. (London, 1966–85). For more recent arguments that emphasize the role of Christianity and the continuity between medieval and modern anti-Semitism see David Berger, ed., *History and Hate: The Dimensions of Anti-Semitism* (Philadelphia, 1986) and the two recent publications by Gavin L. Langmuir, *History, Religion, and Anti-Semitism* (Berkeley, 1990) and *Toward a Definition of Anti-Semitism* (Berkeley, 1990).

3. See Miri Rubin, *Corpus Christi: The Eucharist in Late Medieval Culture* (Cambridge, 1991) esp. pp. 334ff.

4. On the interchangeability between the host and the Christ Child see R. Po-chia Hsia, *The Myth of Ritual Murder: Jews and Magic in Reformation Germany* (New Haven, 1988), pp. 54–56.

5. On Christian polemics against Jews see Joshua Trachtenberg, *The Devil and the Jews* (New Haven, 1943) and Jeremy Cohen, *The Friars and the Jews: The Evolution of Medieval Anti-Judaism* (Ithaca, 1982).

6. Carlo Ginzburg, *Storia notturna. Una decifrazione del sabba* (Turin, 1989), p. 279.

7. František Graus, *Pest-Geissler-Judenmorde: Das 14. Jahrhundert als Krisenzeit* (Göttingen, 1987).
8. Hinderbach's title appears in AST APV, SL, C. 69, 1a, fol. 1r.
9. For Hinderbach's biography, see Armando Costa, *I Vescovi di Trento* (Trent, 1977), pp. 121–25; Alfred A. Strnad, "Johannes Hinderbach," in *Neue Deutsche Biographie* (Berlin, 1974), vol. 10 (1974), pp. 538–39.
10. Otto Stolz, *Die Ausbreitung des Deutschtums in Südtirol im Lichte der Urkunden,* 2 vol. (Munich, 1927–28), 1: 84. In the Tirol itself, the population of the Upper Inntal more than doubled between 1427 and 1615; see Hermann Wopfner, *Bergbauernbuch: Von Arbeit und Leben des Tiroler Bergbauern in Vergangenheit und Gegenwart* (Innsbruck, 1954), 1: 2, 225.
11. Stolz, *Ausbreitung,* 1: 95–96; 2: 308–09. Felix Fabri, a monk from Ulm, passed through the Trent area on his way to and from the Holy Land. For his descriptions of Trent see his travelogue *Fratris Felicis Fabri Evagatorium in terrae sanctae, arabiae et egypti peregrinationem,* (Stuttgart, 1843), 1: 74; for his descriptions of the Alps and the journey from Venice to Ulm see *Evagatorium,* Bibliothek der literarischen Vereins in Stuttgart, 2–4 (Stuttgart, 1849), 3: 441–61. For a historical-anthropological analysis of ethnicity and economy in the Alpine region see Pier Paolo Viazzo, *Upland Communities: Environment, Population and Social Structure in the Alps since the Sixteenth Century* (Cambridge, 1989).
12. Alfred Strnad, "Personalità, famiglia, carriera ecclesiastica di Giovanni Hinderbach prima dell'episcopato," in Iginio Rogger, ed., *Il Principe Vescovo Giovanni Hinderbach (1465–1486) fra tardo medioevo e umanesimo: Incontro di studio, Trento, 2–6 ottobre 1989.* Trent, forthcoming.
13. For the fifteenth and sixteenth centuries, the proportion of canons in Trent was two-thirds German and one-third Italian. See AST, APV, ST, C. 27, p. xxxv.
14. Biblioteca Comunale di Trento. Manuscript no. 828. This is an eighteenth-century copy of the original compact, both in German.
15. For Sigismund see *Biographisches Wörterbuch zur Deutschen Geschichte,* ed. Karl Bosl et al., (Munich, 1975), cols. 3: 2659–60. For the most recent biography see Wilhelm Baum, *Sigmund der Münzreiche: Zur Geschichte Tirols und der habsburgischen Länder im Spätmittelalter* (Bozen, 1987). For the political history of Trent, see Aldo Stella, "I principati vescovili di Trento e Bressanone," in *I Ducati padani, Trento e Trieste,* vol. 17 of *Storia d'Italia,* (Turin, 1979), pp. 510–34. For the conflict between Sigismund and Nicolaus Cusanus, see Otto Stolz, *Geschichte des Landes Tirols* (Innsbruck, 1955), 1: 494–505; Baum, *Sigmund der Münzreiche,* pp. 125–44, 177–90.
16. The "Expositio Canonis Missae" is the second work copied in a manuscript that contains these additional writings: Jacopo de Varazze's "Golden Legends";

a work by Heinrich von Friemar; an anonymous work on the Decalogue; a pseudo-Bonaventure; Jean Gerson's "De arte audiendi confessiones"; and two works by Nicolaus von Dinkelsbühl (a student of Langenstein at Vienna), "Sermones de corporis Christi" and "Sermones de sanctis." Prepared around 1448, the manuscript is in the Biblioteca comunale, Trent, ms. 1573. See *"Pro Bibliotheca Erigenda"* no. 11, pp. 71–73.

17. Langenstein's "Lectura super prologis Bibliae" and "Commentarii super Genesi" are copied in two manuscripts together with the "Tractatus de supersticionibus," falsely attributed to Langenstein but actually composed by Nicolaus Magni de Iawor. Biblioteca comunale, Trent, mss. 1557–1558. See *"Pro Biblotheca Erigenda,"* no. 19, pp. 84–88.

18. The passage on the University of Vienna by Aeneas Silvius reads: "Scola quoque hic est liberalium artium ac theologie et iuris pontificii, noua tamen et ab papa concessa. Magnus studentum numerus eo confluit, ex hungaria et alamanie. . . . Duos hic claruisse compertum habeo prestantes theologos henri cum de Hassia, qui parisiens edoctus, huc in primordio universitatis advolavit, primusque cathedram rexit, ac plurima volumina notatu digna conscripsit." Hinderbach's marginal note reads: "Magister heinricus de Hassia: hic fuit ex genere meo materno, vt ab auia mea que erat sororis eius filia de villa langenstein." Biblioteca comunale, Trent, ms. W 109, c. 39v, reproduced in *"Pro Bibliotheca Erigenda,"* no. 37, p. 127.

19. In the same manuscript with the notation on Heinrich von Langenstein, Hinderbach also made many marginal comments on the text of Aeneas Silvius' "De librorum educatione." On the composition of this work, Hinderbach wrote: "Ego quoque non mediocris fui huius operis instigator." Biblioteca comunale, Trent, ms. W 109, c. 2r; see *"Pro Bibliotheca Erigenda,"* p. 128.

20. Michael H. Shank, *"Unless You Believe, You Shall Not Understand": Logic, University, and Society in Late Medieval Vienna* (Princeton, 1988), pp. 9, 146.

21. "De ideomate Ebraico" and "Tractatus de contractibus," see Shank, *Vienna,* p. 149.

22. See David Berger, "Jewish-Christian Polemics," *The Encyclopedia of Religion,* ed. Mircea Eliade (New York, 1987), pp. 389–95.

23. Cited in Shank, *Vienna,* pp. 159–60.

24. Shank, *Vienna,* pp. 188–89.

25. Shank, *Vienna,* pp. 191–98.

26. Katherine Walsh, "Eredità tardomedievale e germi dell'Umanesimo nella formazione spirituale di Giovanni Hinderbach," in Rogger, *Hinderbach.* On anti-Jewish polemics in quattrocento Italy see Gianfranco Fioravanti, "Polemiche antiguidaiche nell'Italia del Quattrocento: Un tentativo di interpretazione globale," *Quaderni Storici* no. 64, vol. 22:1 (1987), pp. 19–37.

CHAPTER TWO: THE JEWISH COMMUNITY

1. Until the seventeenth century, Jewish communities in northern Italy were predominantly Ashkenazic. See Moses A. Shulvass, *The Jews in the World of the Renaissance*, trans. Elvin Kose (Leiden, 1973), pp. 15–20. For the fifteenth-century expulsions in German imperial cities see Markus J. Wenninger, *Man bedarf keinen Juden mehr: Ursachen und Hintergründe ihrer Vertreibung aus der deutschen Reichsstädten im 15. Jahrhundert* (Cologne, 1981).

2. On a family reconstitution of the Ashkenazim see Kenneth R. Stow, "The Jewish Family in the Rhineland in the High Middle Ages: Form and Function," *American Historical Review* 92 (1987), pp. 1085–1110.

3. YM, fol. 47.

4. Manuscript record of the trial against the Jews of Trent ("Prozess gegen die Juden von Trient"), New York, Yeshiva University Library, fols. 19–21. Hereafter cited as YM.

5. On the retention of Ashkenazic names, see Shulvass, *Jews in the World of the Renaissance,* pp. 34–35.

6. This document is published by Giuseppe Menestrina in his "Gli Ebrei a Trento," *Tridentum. Rivista di studi scientifici* (October 1903), pp. 307–08, 308 n. 1.

7. Menestrina, "Gli Ebrei a Trento," pp. 304–07.

8. YM, fol. 596.

9. YM, fols. 583–84.

10. YM, fol. 131.

11. YM, fols. 194–95.

12. YM, fol. 191.

13. YM, fol. 201.

14. YM, fol. 191.

15. YM, fol. 533.

16. YM, fol. 103.

17. YM, fol. 324.

18. YM, fol. 182.

19. YM, fols. 217, 222, 240, 303, 535–36, 569.

20. YM, fols. 499, 501.

21. YM, fol. 506.

22. YM, fols. 250, 304.

23. YM, fol. 289.

24. YM, fols. 304, 313.

25. YM, fol. 289.

26. YM, fol. 296.

27. YM, fols. 14–15.
28. YM, fol. 78.
29. YM, fol. 214.
30. YM, fol. 93.
31. YM, fols. 214, 227–28.
32. YM, fol. 159.
33. YM, fol. 10 names Engel's father as Salomon of Bern, whereas the Vatican ms. gives the name as Salomon of Verona. Cf. *Processi,* doc. 5, p. 114.
34. YM, fol. 568.
35. YM, fol. 546.
36. YM, fols. 555, 568.
37. YM, fols. 317, 335, 342. In the Latin mss. Friaul is written "Friolo."
38. YM, fols. 14–15, 253, 270.
39. *Processi,* doc. 108, p. 401.
40. YM, fols. 33–36.
41. YM, fols. 396–97.
42. YM, fols. 350, 379.
43. YM, fol. 75.
44. YM, fols. 371, 381.
45. YM, fol. 371.
46. YM, fol. 379.
47. The reconstruction of the physical appearance and social makeup of the neighborhood comes from the testimonies of Blond Gretchen; Margaritha, wife of Hans Lederer; Roper the tailor; Wolf Holzknecht; and Johannes the Schweizer. See YM, fols. 19–22; *Processi,* doc. 15, p. 128; doc. 16, p. 130; doc. 108, pp. 394–404; doc. 112–113, pp. 407–08.
48. On the relationships between Jewish physicians and Christian patients see Robert A. Jütte, "Jewish Physicians in Early Modern Europe," in R. Po-chia Hsia and Hartmut Lehmann, eds., *In and Out of the Ghetto: Jewish-Gentile Relations in Late Medieval and Early Modern Germany* (Cambridge, forthcoming).
49. On Bernardino and Trent, see Giuseppe Menestrina, "Gli Ebrei a Trento," *Tridentum* 6 (1903), p. 374; and Gemma Volli, "I 'Processi Tridentini' e il Culto del Beato Simone da Trento," *Il Ponte* 11 (November 1963). On Franciscan preachings supporting the Monti di Pietà and attacking the Jews, see Renata Segre, "I Monti di Pietà e i Banchi Ebraici," *Rivista storica Italiana* 90: 4 (1978), pp. 818–33.

CHAPTER THREE: THE INQUEST

1. Testimony of Seligman the cook, 28 March 1475, YM, fol. 75.
2. Testimony of Anna, 28 March 1475 and 1 March 1476, YM, fols. 582–83.

3. Testimony of Tobias, 7 and 17 April 1475, YM, fols. 168, 177; testimony of Sara, 4 November 1475, YM, fols. 483–85.

4. Testimony of Tobias, 3 April 1475, YM, fol. 166.

5. Testimony of Isaac, 29 October 1475, YM, fol. 258.

6. Testimony of Lazarus, 13 April 1475, YM, fols. 320–21.

7. Testimony of Tobias, 3 April 1475, YM, fols. 161–65.

8. Testimony of Sara, 3 November 1475, YM, fol. 480.

9. Testimony of Tobias, 3 April 1475, YM, fol. 165.

10. Testimonies of Sara, 3 November 1475, and Moses, 28 November 1475, YM, fols. 480, 306–07.

11. Testimonies of Sara, 3 November 1475, and Seligman, 27 March 1475, YM, fols. 481, 93.

12. Testimony of Sara, 3 November 1475, YM, fol. 481.

13. Testimony of Israel, 19 April 1475, YM, fol. 393. Israel described the angry conversation between Tobias and Salomon; he told of Salomon going into Tobias' room, saying: "Ich glaub nit dass die Juden sollich ding thuen den hat Thobian da gestrafft vnd het gesprochen, du solt mein melichtz, das ist redner, tülmatsch oder vorsprech nit sein, und het zu dem Salomon gesprochen aber Du solt nit sprechen das Du glaubst dass dy Juden das nit thuen, du solt das furgewiss sagen, sy thuen des nit." According to Gütlein, Engel's sister, Tobias was an angry man and had dismissed many servants; see her testimony of 27 March 1476, YM, fol. 571.

14. Testimony of Young Moses, 28 November 1475, YM, fols. 306–07, 314–15.

15. Testimonies of Seligman, 27 March 1475, and Joaff, 31 March 1485, YM, fols. 93, 215.

16. Testimony of Tobias, 3 April 1475, YM, fol. 164.

17. Testimony of Isaac, 30 November 1475, YM, fol. 280.

18. Süsslein's lament was reported by Moses: "Wee mir, sÿ werden mir mein sün nemen vnd werden die tauffen. Het ich nür den sun nit so het ich kainen smerzen. Do het er [Moses] sy ermant sy solt so ser nit waynen, es wär villeicht so pöß nit als sy maynet" (YM, fol. 360).

19. This reconstruction of events is based on the testimonies of Isaac, 30 November 1475 and of his father, Moses of Bamberg, 31 October 1475, YM, fols. 280 and 359–61, respectively.

20. Testimony of Moses of Bamberg, 10 November 1475, YM, fol. 377.

21. Testimony of Schönlein, 3 November 1475, YM, fol. 515.

22. YM, fol. 9–10; Processi, doc. 5, pp. 112–15.

23. "Vnd offenbar und bewert ist dar die erschlagen leut, in gegenbart wer man schlechter oder mörder pluetten," YM, fol. 10. This popular belief was a familiar charge in blood libels; see Hsia, Myth of Ritual Murder, p. 202.

24. Testimonies of Schönlein, 4 February 1476, and Anna, 9 March 1476, YM, fols. 532, 594–95, respectively.
25. Testimony of Lazarus, 20 November 1475, YM, fol. 330.
26. Testimony of Israel, 18 November 1475, YM, fol. 420.
27. I have followed the Italianized and Latinized names as recorded in the Latin manuscripts. The YM (fol. 11) gives their names in German as "Magister Erzengel von Baldum" and "Magister Johan Mathias." The name of the lawyer was "Her Wolfan der Kaiserlichen Rechten Gelerer."
28. For the medical testimonies see YM, fols. 12–13; *Processi,* docs. 6–8, pp. 115–20.
29. YM, fols. 14–15.
30. YM, fol. 16; *Processi,* doc. 10, pp. 121–22.
31. YM, fols. 16–17.
32. YM, fols. 18–19.
33. Margaritha's testimony was given great weight by the magistrates, as reflected by its centrality in the narrative of the trial record. See YM, fols. 19–21, "Kuntschafft der gelben Grett die ettwan auch ein kind verlor vnd bey den Juden gefunden het." See also AST, APV, SL, C. 69, no. 1b, fol. 7v; *Processi,* doc. 15, pp. 127–29.
34. YM, fol. 22; *Processi,* doc. 16, pp. 130–31. The importance of the statements of de Feltre and the two Margarithas is highlighted in the Yeshiva manuscript by this authorial comment, written in red ink immediately following the transcripts of the statements written in black ink: "Also endt sich hie ettlich mercklich anzaigen wider die Juden, von des mords wegen, des saligen kindleins und martrers saind Simon, durch dieselben falschen Juden in der löblichen Stat zu Trennt vnmenschlich ermordet."

CHAPTER FOUR: THE TORTURE CHAMBER

1. The Statute Alessandrino of 1425 (book 2, chapter 17) specified that "qui gastaldiones si Potestas vellet excedere modum torquendo, refraenare intentionem Potestatis debeant." In the same article, it admonished "quod Potestas vel alius officialis non possit nec valeat aliquem ad torturam ponere sine praesentia dictorum gastaldionum vel duorum consulum Civitatis, sub poena viginti quinque librarum, pro qualibet vice, qua contrafactum fuerit per ipsum Potestatem vel officialem, auferenda de suo salario et applicanda Camerae Fiscali in tortum." Quoted in Menestrina, "Gli Ebrei a Trento," p. 397.
2. For the interrogations of "the Other Seligman," see YM, fols. 93–109; *Processi,* docs. 24–32, pp. 153–73.

3. *Processi,* doc. 24, p. 154; YM, fol. 94: "Da aber der potestat sach das er dy warhait nit hellen wolt, hieß er den emplößen pindten vnd auffziehen."

4. YM, fol. 95.

5. For the interrogations of Seligman the cook, see YM, fols. 75–91; *Processi,* docs. 17–23, pp. 133–51.

6. In the Vatican ms. Metzger's name is given as Nicolaus Claus, *Processi,* p. 134.

7. YM, fol. 77.

8. YM, fol. 78.

9. YM, fol. 131; *Processi,* doc. 45, p. 206.

10. YM, fol. 111; *Processi,* doc. 35, pp. 179–80.

11. For Samuel's interrogations, see YM, fols. 24–74; *Processi,* docs. 59–69, pp. 233–79. The sessions of 31 March 1475 are recorded in YM, fols. 24–27; *Processi,* pp. 235–37.

12. Interrogations in the YM were recorded in indirect discourse. I have rendered the translations in dialogue form in order to restore a sense of immediacy. Other than supplying the names of the interlocutors, the dialogues are translated into English following the record in the YM as closely as possible.

13. For the interrogations of Joaff, see YM, fols. 214–49; the session of 31 March 1475 is recorded on fols. 214–19.

14. For the interrogations of Engel, see YM, fols. 147–160; *Processi,* docs. 70–81, pp. 281–306. The sessions of 31 March 1475 are recorded in YM, fols. 147–49; *Processi,* docs. 70–71, pp. 281–83.

15. The scribe omitted these testimonies, probably to make the narrative of the ritual murder less complicated and more focused on the Jews. For the testimonies of the Schweizer and Dorothea, see AST, APV, SL, C. 69, no. 1b, fols. 119v–124r, "Processus inquisitionis contra Zanesum Sweyzer, etc." This is a Latin version of the trial records, bound in a folio manuscript. For a rougher copy of the Schweizer's testimony, written in loose folios, see AST, APV, SL, C. 69, no. 4 (II), fol. 199r. See also *Processi,* docs. 106–110, pp. 393–403.

16. Testimony of Dorothea, 31 March 1475, *Processi,* doc. 109, pp. 401–03.

17. On the different land tenures in the German-speaking and Italian-speaking Tirol see Wopfner, *Bergbauernbuch,* 1:3, 469. On wine exports from Trent to the Tirol in the late fifteenth century see Hermann Wopfner, *Die Lage Tirols zu Ausgang des Mittelalters und die Ursachen des Bauernkrieges* (Berlin, 1908), p. 29.

18. There is a discrepancy between the YM and the Vatican ms. as to the date of his release. The YM lists 21 April 1475; the Vatican ms. lists 11 April 1475.

19. For the interrogations of "Roper Snaider" see: AST, APV, SL, C. 69, no. 1b, fols. 124r–126r; AST, APV, SL, C. 69, no. 4 (II), fol. 206v; *Processi,* docs. 111–115, pp. 405–10.

20. *Processi,* doc. 113, pp. 407–08.

21. Testimony of Old Moses, 4 April 1475, YM, fol. 192; *Processi,* doc. 92, p. 350.

22. YM, fols. 131–32; *Processi,* doc. 46, p. 207.
23. YM, fol. 29: "Antwurt er hetts gesagt und man penigt in unrechtlich, da hieß man in zwie springe auff ii oder iii ann hoch da hieng er und sprach, Gott der Helffer, und die Warhait helffen mir, und do er also uff ii Drittel einer stund gehangen was, hieß man in ablassen und füern in vancknuß." See also *Processi,* doc. 61, p. 238.
24. YM, fols. 29–31; *Processi,* doc. 62, pp. 238–39.
25. YM, fols. 149–53; for the session of 8 April 1475, see YM, fols. 150–53; *Processi,* doc. 74, pp. 285–88.
26. YM, fol. 161. For Tobias' interrogation, see YM, fols. 161–90; *Processi,* docs. 82–91, pp. 307–48.
27. YM, fols. 161–67.
28. YM, fol. 168: "Man ließ in nyder, da bedacht er wär schier enwicht oder verdorben vnd als er ein wenig zu innselbs kam, fraget in der potestat der warheit."
29. YM, fols. 169–77.
30. For interrogations of Old Moses, see YM, fols. 191–203; *Processi,* docs. 92–99, pp. 349–74. For the session of 4 April 1475, see YM, fol. 191–93; *Processi,* doc. 92, pp. 349–52.
31. For interrogations of Mayer, see YM, fols. 204–13; *Processi,* docs. 100–105, pp. 375–92.
32. YM, fols. 113–15; *Processi,* doc. 36, pp. 180–85.
33. YM, fols. 79–81. Seligman broke down only after prolonged torture. In the words of the scribe: "Ward vor dem hauptman der benant Saligman durch den potestaten der warhait gefragt, er sprach, er hets gesagt, man schueff in zuem ploßen pindten und auffziehen, und da frag man, er antwurt, last mich hynab, ich wil die warheit sagen, also hengt man und fraget hernyder sein antwurt was. Er hets gesagt, da zach man den hinwider, und ließ in ein klain springen und fragt, er antwurt er hets gesagt vnd wiß nit anders, da ließ man in zainzigen springen zwie, und fragt in also hangenden wie vor, er antwurt alß vor." Finally, Seligman was hoisted up yet again "vnd hueb im ein gluet mit swebel in einer phannen under die nasen." Cf. *Processi,* doc. 18, pp. 136–38.
34. YM, fol. 97; *Processi,* doc. 25, pp. 155–56.
35. YM, fols. 99–100; *Processi,* doc. 26, pp. 156–59.
36. YM, fol. 153: "Hienach bekant er Recht."
37. For Tobias' testimony of 17 April 1475, see YM, fols. 177–89; here, fol. 179. The Vatican ms. gives the date of this session as 19 April 1475. See: *Processi,* doc. 87, pp. 322–31.
38. YM, fol. 182; *Processi,* p. 327.
39. YM, fols. 184–85; *Processi,* p. 328.
40. YM, fols. 187–89; *Processi,* pp. 331ff.

41. YM, fol. 132; *Processi*, doc. 48, pp. 209–10.
42. YM, fol. 135; *Processi*, doc. 49, pp. 210–12.
43. YM, fol. 136; *Processi*, doc. 50, pp. 212–13.
44. YM, fol. 137; *Processi*, doc. 51, pp. 214–16.
45. YM, fols. 139–40; *Processi*, docs. 52–53, pp. 216–18.
46. YM, fols. 205–11; *Processi*, doc. 101, pp. 376–81.
47. YM, fol. 211; *Processi*, p. 381.
48. YM, fols. 205–11, especially 207; *Processi*, p. 378.
49. YM, fols. 132–40; *Processi*, docs. 52–53, pp. 216–18.
50. YM, fols. 118–19; *Processi*, doc. 37, pp. 185–87.
51. The sentence means literally, "Thus it was done to the God of the Christians, who is not a true god, and that gentlemen are arriving on horses and on a nag." The words in the Venetian-Padua dialects can be found in Gasparo Patriarchi, comp., *Vocabolario Veneziano e padovano co'termini e modi corrispondenti Toscani* (Padua, 1821). Quaglioni and Esposito suggest that the words are a garbled version of a passage from Exodus 15:18–20; see *Processi*, p. 442n.
52. YM, fol. 120 (in red ink): "Hie zemercken wie offt er mit seinen worten wexelt und hiewider spricht er alle vorgeschribne ding, darumb man im von newen darauff fragt."
53. YM, fol. 121; *Processi*, doc. 38, p. 188.
54. YM, fols. 122–23; *Processi*, doc. 39, pp. 189–90.
55. For the interrogations of Lazarus, see YM, fols. 317–49. For the sessions of 12 and 13 April 1475, see fols. 317–21. See fol. 320 for the quotation "Er antwurt, sagt mir was sol ich sagen, sol wil ich es sagen."
56. For the interrogations of Isaac, see YM, fols. 253–86. For the session of 11 April 1475, see fol. 253.
57. For the interrogations of Moses of Bamberg, see YM, fols. 350–88. For the session of 14 April 1475, see fols. 350–51. To his reply "peynigt mich nur vast daß ich pald sterb," the response was "man ließ in hangen, man zach in höher."
58. YM, fol. 250. For the interrogations of Young Moses, see fols. 250–316.
59. For the interrogations of Israel (Wolfgang), see YM, fols. 389–477. The quotation is from the session of 12 April 1475, fol. 390: "Wie wol die teutschen sprechen, die Juden tötten cristen kinder, so war es doch nit war."

CHAPTER FIVE: "BLESSED SIMON MARTYR"

1. AST, APV, SL, C. 69, no. 10.
2. For Zovenzoni's connections to Venetian humanists see Margaret L. King, *Venetian Humanism in an Age of Patrician Dominance* (Princeton, 1986), p. 232 nn. 67, 69; pp. 267, 369, 386, 445, 448. For his biography see B. Ziliotto, *Raffaele*

Zovenzoni: La vita, i carmi (Trieste, 1950). For a general discussion of the reception of Simon's cult in humanist circles and humanist hagiography after 1475 see Anna Esposito, "La stereotipo dell'omicidio rituali nei processi tridenti e il culto del 'beato' Simone," *Processi,* pp. 81ff.

3. AST, APV, SL, C. 69, no. 5.
4. Divina, *Storia,* 2:228.
5. AST, APV, SL, C. 69, no. 1d. This batch of papers contains sheets of account, kept in Latin and German, recording various dates and sums; the earliest date is 23 April 1475. The handwriting is that of Johannes Hinderbach.
6. Josef E. Scherer, *Die Rechtsverhältnisse der Juden in den deutsch-Österreichischen Ländern* (Leipzig, 1901), p. 602.
7. From "Carmen Joannis Calphurni ad Joannem Hinderbachium," quoted in Benedetto Bonelli, *Dissertazione apologetica sul martirio del Beato Simone da Trento nell'anno 1475 dagli ebrei ucciso* (Trent, 1747).
8. Quoted in Menestrina, "Gli Ebrei a Trento," 392, n. 1.

> Surgite pontifices, tuque O Sanctissime Caesar,
> Vosque Duces, Regesque, precor, populique patresque
> Qui Christum colitis, Christum qui sanguine lavit
> Erroris quicquid nostri admisere parentes.
> Stringite fulmineos enses, trucidate nephandum
> Iudaicum nomen, totaque expellite terra.
> Hoc genus in terris, genus hoc precor esse sinetis!
> Syxte pater prohibe: prohibe, Federice, cruorem
> Qui nostrum sitiunt nostris simul urbibus esse
> Amplius. Imperii dux Sigismunde latini,
> Nunc animos ostende tuos, tu porrige flammas
> in quibus hebreum scelus oxcuratur, et insons
> Sanguis apud superos te praedicet ut mea laurus
> Praesidiumque meum pater Hinderbache Ioannes.
> Perge vetat nemo quin perdas perfida verpos
> Corpora: quin rapidis cinerem des spargere ventis.
> Hoc iubet ipse deus: iubet hoc tua sancta potestas,
> Iustitia, pietasque, fides et candida virtus
> Quae te celicolis est donatura catervis.

9. Quoted in Menestrina, "Gli Ebrei a Trento," 392, n. 1.

> Ad tumulum quisque, meum accurrit aeger, abibit
> Sospes et incolumis cecus, claudusque et alter
> Quicumque misero morbo laborat
> Ut pateat cunctis scelus, gens impia, tuum.

Non satis est aurum, gemmas, diversi generis opes
Gentis christicolae devoras: corrodis undique pronos
Et sanguinem sitis, bibis et azima spargis
Et Christi fidem gentemque ludibrio spernis
Cunctisque maledico blasphemas ore diebus
Et nobis improperas, nostro qui sanguine vivis.
Insurgant Reges, Duces, proceresque Tyranni,
Pontifices sacri, Dives et populi omnes,
Huius nephandae in caput concurrite gentis
Totamque perpropere cunctis de finibus orbis
Nominis christicolum procul iam pellite canes.

10. The manuscript by Tiberino, Ms. N. E 1527 in the Biblioteca Queriniana, Brescia, has been published by Frumenzio Ghetta in his *Fra Bernardino Tomitano da Feltre e gli Ebrei di Trento nel 1475* (Trent, n.d.), pp. 40–45. I am indebted to Father Ghetta for providing me with a copy of his booklet.

11. For the iconography of the Mater Dolorosa, see Hsia, *Myth of Ritual Murder*, pp. 58–59 and figure 6.

12. Tiberino's lines : "Tempus erat quo prima quies humana reficit pectora atque quiescebant voces hominumque canumque." Compare *Aeneid* 2.268–69: "Tempus erat quo prima quies mortalibus aegris incipit et dono diuum gratissima serpit." This observation is made by Diego Quaglioni in his "Propaganda antiebriaca e polemiche di curia," in *Un pontificato ed una città: Sisto IV (1471–1484)*, (Rome, 1986), pp. 243–66; here, 255.

13. The full description of the little boy giving his soul reads: "Iam plus quam per horam miserandus puer terribili duraverat in supplicio et interdicto spiritu colapsis viribus in testes, et inclinato capite sanctum Domino reddidit spiritum." Compare John 19:30 on Christ's passion: "Et inclinato capite tradidit spiritum." The following sentence from Tiberino, "Purpureus veluti cum flos succisus arato languescit moriens lapsaque papavera collo dimisere caput pluvie cum forte gravantur," is almost identical to *Aeneid* 9.435–37. See Quaglioni, "Propaganda antiebraica," pp. 254–55.

14. "Pro bibliotheca erigenda," pp. 23–24. The German title was *Geschichte des zu Trient ermordeten Christenkindes*.

15. The poem, "Sum puer ille Simon," is reprinted in Bonelli, *Dissertazione*, pp. 88–89, note a.

16. Hsia, *Myth of Ritual Murder*, 44–45.

17. The title was *L'aspra crudeltà del Turco a quegli di Caffa*. See *The Imprint Catalog in the Rare Book Division*, Research Division, New York Public Library. (Boston, 1979), 19: 558. The other three titles are listed in *"Pro bibliotheca erigenda,"* 23.

18. Leo Steinberg, *The Sexuality of Christ in Renaissance Art and in Modern Oblivion* (New York, 1983).

19. YM, fol. 332.
20. On the connections between forms of popular piety and anti-Semitism in late medieval Europe, see R. Po-chia Hsia, "Die Sakralisierung der Gesellschaft: Blutfrömmigkeit und Verehrung der Heiligen Familie vor der Reformation," in *Kommunalisierung und Christianisierung: Voraussetzungen und Folgen der Reformation 1400–1600*, Zeitschrift für Historische Forschung, Beiheft 9 (Berlin, 1989), pp. 57–75

CHAPTER SIX: THEATER OF DEATH

1. Divina, *Storia,* 1: 98.
2. YM, fol. 31; *Processi,* doc. 63, p. 240.
3. YM, fols. 31–32; *Processi,* doc. 63, p. 241.
4. YM, fol. 38: "Merckt man ach die sin ach und uneer cristi in fluech und rach pett uber die Cristen."
5. YM, fol. 38. The Hebrew was probably copied from the Haggadah, confiscated by the magistrates. I am indebted to David Berger of Brooklyn College for pointing out that some of the Hebrew letters were garbled by the copyist. For explanation of the Hebrew transliteration see *Processi,* p. 443n.
6. YM, fols. 39–43; *Processi,* doc. 64, pp. 250–53.
7. YM, fols. 43–47; *Processi,* pp. 253–56.
8. YM, fol. 48; *Processi,* p. 253.
9. YM, fols. 49–51; *Processi,* pp. 255–56.
10. YM, fols. 52–54; *Processi,* doc. 65, pp. 256–58.
11. YM, fol. 143: "Hienach sagt er recht die warhait und gentz geleich mit den anderen."
12. YM, fols. 124–26; *Processi,* doc. 40, pp. 191–93.
13. YM, fols. 194–95; *Processi,* doc. 93, p. 352.
14. YM, fols. 195–200; *Processi,* doc. 94, pp. 353–59.
15. YM, fols. 101–02; *Processi,* doc. 27, p. 160.
16. YM, fols. 55–56: "Er wüst vnd verstuend wol, das der obgenant Samuel ein tüttscher wär, vnd wol tütsch vnd wellisch kundt . . . yedoch zu merer erklärung vnd größer verstentigkeit schueff er mit dem Notari, daß er Conten von Terlacko . . . in tüttsch sagen wolt alles das in der nachgeschriben frag in latin begriffen, vnd durch den Notari ufgelegt wurd, daß er auch herwiderumb truelich vnd mit gueter gewissen, wie vor dem potestaten vnd dem notarei in latein sagen wolt, alles das der bemelt Samuel in tüttsch daruff antwurten wurd." Cf. *Processi,* doc. 66, p. 259.
17. YM, fol. 55: "Das ist deß Potestat gerichtsfrag, wie er die uß dem obgenant Samuel Juden vorgeschribner bekanntnuß genomen, und geformiert hat, nach des rechtens und irer satzung gewonheit die man dann dem selben Samuel vor

gericht gelesen und in tütsch ußgelegt hat, daruff er öffenlich daselbs verholln
und mit seinem ayd vor gericht bestät hat alß sich hie nach vinden wirt."
18. YM, fols. 58–60.
19. YM, fols. 62–71; *Processi,* doc. 66, pp. 261–66, contains a detailed recounting
of the alleged ritual murder.
20. YM, fols. 104–05, 114, 201–02; *Processi,* docs. 30, 56, 96, pp. 165–67, 224–25,
365–66.
21. YM, fols. 202–03; *Processi,* doc. 97, p. 366.
22. YM, fols. 74, 128, 189–90; *Processi,* docs. 44, 69, 81, 91, pp. 204, 279, 306, 348.
23. YM, fols. 145–46, 212–13; *Processi,* docs. 58, 105, pp. 231, 392.
24. YM, fols. 88–91, 108–09; *Processi,* docs. 33–34, pp. 175–77.

CHAPTER SEVEN: THE APOSTOLIC COMMISSIONER

1. See Quaglioni, "Il procedimento inquisitorio contro gli Ebrei di Trento,"
Processi, pp. 38–51, and Esposito, "Lo stereotipo dell'omicidio rituale," *Processi,*
pp. 81–93.
2. AST, SL, C. 69, no. 25. For a succinct introduction to the events and sources
discussed in this chapter, see Baptista dei Giudici, *Apologia Iudaeorum: Invectiva
contra Platinam. Propaganda antiebraica e polemiche di Curia durante il Pontificato di
Sisto IV (1471–1484)* ed. Diego Quaglioni (Rome, 1987). Hereafter cited as
Quaglioni, *Apologia Iudaeorum.*
3. AST, APV, SL, C. 69, no. 29. See Quaglioni, *Apologia Iudaeorum,* pp. 15–16.
4. Quaglioni, *Apologia Iudaeorum,* pp. 38–40.
5. Quaglioni, *Apologia Iudaeorum,* p.54. Dei Giudici on the reasons for his own
appointment: "Cuius doctrinam et vite integritatem et ipse sanctissimus dominus noster sepe in minoribus exploratas et cognitas habuit . . . et omnes
norunt quali fama sit versatus et continue versetur in curia, qui etiam sepe
contra Iudeos et predicavit et scripsit, et . . . nunquam in omni vita sua vel
semel cum aliquo Iudeo aut comedit aut bibit."
6. Quaglioni, *Apologia Iudaeorum,* p. 142.
7. There are four sources, deposited in archives in Trent and at the Vatican, all
edited and published by Quaglioni. The first is a nine-point accusation sent to
Rome by Hinderbach after the return of the apostolic commissioner, entitled
"Informatio facti in causa innocentis infantuli Simonis Tridentini, a perfidis
Iudeis in contumeliam et obprobrium passionis domini nostri Iesu Christi
crudeliter interempti." Dei Giudici's defense, "Confutaciones vere et solu-
ciones falsarum obiectionum per Tridentinos ac eorum fautores contra dominum episcopum Ventimilliensem, commissarium apostolicum porrectarum,
per defensores veritatis et honoris sedis apostolice et ipsius commissarii ex-

hibite," written in response to Hinderbach, appears in Quaglioni's volume as *Apologia Iudaeorum*. The third document is Hinderbach's objection to Dei Giudici's response, "Responsiones ad obiecta domini commissarii Vigintimiliensis." These three sources contain detailed accounts of the commissioner's sojourn in Trent. The fourth document, "Invectiva Baptiste episcopi Intemeliensis contra Platinam," an attack composed by Dei Giudici against the papal librarian, a Hinderbach partisan, contains a section that is relevant to the episode in Trent.

8. Quaglioni, *Apologia Iudaeorum*, pp. 142–44.
9. Quaglioni, *Apologia Iudaeorum*, p. 104.
10. The letter is reprinted in P. Ghinzoni, "San Simone di Trento 1475," *Archivio Storico Lombardo* 16 (1889). 140–42. Cited in *Processi*, p. 80.
11. Quaglioni, *Apologia Iudaeorum*, pp. 60, 146.
12. Quaglioni, *Apologia Iudaeorum*, pp. 74–76.
13. Quaglioni, *Apologia Iudaeorum*, p. 158: "Et cum ipse dominus commissarius omni studio conaretur liberacionem illorum, tam apud dominum principem quam etiam dominum episcopum, prout etiam postea Roveredi mandaverat sub penis et censuris illos relaxari, contra protestaciones suas factas et contra tenorem brevis apostolici, quo continebatur quod relaxari deberent si culpa carerent, etc. Timebatur si illis loqueretur ne aliquod signum, ipse vel sui, ipsis Iudeis darent, quo obstinaciores redditi fuissent; quoniam semper dixerant: 'Veniet unus qui nos liberabit.'"
14. AST, APV, SL, C. 69, no. 184, quoted in Quaglioni, "Propaganda antiebraica," pp. 25–52, n. 31, and Quaglioni, *Apologia Iudaeorum*, pp. 54–56: "Sed idem Tridentinus episcopus fecit illi parare pessimum et inhonestum hospicium vicinum suo castro, in quo cum magna incomoditate et propria expensa stetit diebus xxii, semper infirmus propter malam cameram, que erat humidissima et in quam desuper pluebat, quia e superiori loco tota erat aperta; usque adeo quod fuit necesse ipsum pluribus noctibus exire de lecto, propter pluvias que passim per cameram fluebant. Erant etiam ibi fetores colluvionum, letaminis et imundiciarum; et in quo loco nemo poterat ad eum accedere et occulta revelare, nec ipse officium suum exequi, tanta erat custodia que per homines episcopi Tridentini fiebat."
15. Quaglioni, *Apologia Iudaeorum*, p. 60: "Et quia multi de populo, qui furore magis quam ratione et magis temeritate quam devotione movebantur, minabantur per angulos civitatis ipsi commissario mortem, nisi ista miracula et assertum martirium confirmaret."
16. Quaglioni, *Apologia Iudaeorum*, p. 62.
17. Quaglioni, *Apologia Iudaeorum*, pp. 158–60.
18. Quaglioni, *Apologia Iudaeorum*, p. 130.
19. Quaglioni, *Apologia Iudaeorum*, pp. 64–66: "Secessit in locum tutum et

ydoneum, Roveredi . . . sub protectione illustrissimi ducalis domini Vene-
ciarum, ubi semper ministratur et ministrata fuit iusticia, necque occiduntur
insontes nec depredantur Christiani Iudeos, ut fit Tridenti."

20. Quaglioni, *Apologia Iudaeorum,* p. 132: "Illi [Jewish advocates] replicaver-
unt. . . . quod volebant defendere non mortuos, qui resurgere non possunt,
sed veritatem; et quod volebant defendere causam vivorum non solum incar-
ceratorum, sed etiam eorum qui sunt per totum orbem, que per istos processus si sic probarentur, periclitaretur: quia in processibus dicunt contineri
quod confessi sunt omnes Hebreos de decennio in decennium, et precipue in
anno iubilei, Christianorum utantur sanguine puerorum."

21. Quaglioni, *Apologia Iudaeorum,* pp. 134–36.

22. AST, APV, SL, C. 69, no. 22.

23. Bonelli, *Dissertazione,* 245a; Divina, *Storia,* 2:96–98.

24. AST, APV, SL, C. 69, no. 45.

25. AST, APV, SL, C. 69, no. 54.

26. AST, APV, SL, C. 69, no. 58. This document was missing from the archive
when I requested it on 24 September 1988. For the Endingen trial, see Hsia,
Myth of Ritual Murder, chapter 2.

27. AST, APV, SL, C. 69, no. 43.

28. AST, APV, SL, C. 69, no. 276.

29. AST, APV, SL, C. 69, no. 50.

30. AST, APV, SL, C. 69, no. 27.

31. AST, APV, SL, C. 69, no. 28.

32. AST, APV, SL, c. 69, no. 32.

33. See correspondence concerning Anzelino between Captain Jakob de Sporo of
Trent and Ludovico Zvivinus, podestà of Rovereto. AST, APV, SL, C. 69, no. 49
and 51. On the charges and counter-charges over Anzelino's interrogation
between Hinderbach and Dei Giudici, see Quaglioni, *Apologia Iudaeorum,*
pp. 78–80, 150–52.

34. AST, APV, SL, C. 69, no. 55.

35. AST, APV, SL, C. 69, nos. 56, 59.

36. Divina, *Storia,* 2: 307–08.

37. AST, APV, SL, C. 69, no. 30.

38. AST, APV, SL, C. 69, no. 20.

39. AST, APV, SL, C. 69, no. 21.

40. AST, APV, SL, C. 69, nos. 38, 39.

41. AST, APV, SL, C. 69, no. 41.

42. AST, APV, SL, C. 69, nos. 42, 43.

43. In 1477, Hinderbach accused Dei Giudici of "losing" the souls of the Jewish
children, when they were released and not baptized along with their mothers
in Trent. See Quaglioni, *Apologia Iudaeorum,* p. 158.

44. Divina, *Storia*, 2: 124–25.
45. Quaglioni, *Apologia Iuaeorum*, pp. 104–06.

CHAPTER EIGHT: AN ETHNOGRAPHY OF BLOOD

1. Ludwig von Pastor does not mention Trent at all in his discussion of the reign of Sixtus IV. See his *History of the Popes from the Close of the Middle Ages*, vol. 4 (St. Louis, 1902).
2. AST, APV, SL, C. 69, no. 3, ad. fol. 4; The letter, really a note, is folded and inserted into the binding of a transcript of the interrogation of Israel (Wolfgang): "Sigismund rd: Getreuer lieben. Wir emphelhen dir daz du den Juden vnd Judin so du in Vennkhnuß hast freilelich recht wie sich gebüret ergeen laßest todt ergeen zulaßen schaffest vnd waz dann zu recht erkannt wirdet dem also nackkomest, daran tust du vnnser cristliche maynung. Geben an Meran an Fritag nach Sand Gallen tag anno domini a. lxxv. Vnnserm getrewen liebn Jacobn Spaw;r vnnser hauptman zu Triendt." (Punctuation added.) In his discussion of the Trent ritual murder trial, Wilhelm Baum seems unaware of Sigismund's direct role, cf. his *Sigmund der Münzreiche*, pp. 378–81.
3. For Isaac's interrogations, see YM, fols. 256–86. Here, see fol. 257: "Man hengt vnd ließ in sitzen vnd fraget. Antwurt ja west ich was ich sagen solt, ich saget es gern, do er also ein weyl sass, vnd saget nichts, hieß man in auffziehen."
4. YM, fol. 259: "Er sprach er wolt dy warheit hindten sagen vnd west nichts vnd west wol das er sterven muest."
5. For Lazarus's interrogations, see YM, fols. 321–49. Here, fol. 331: "Man sprach er solt alles sagen das da geredt vnd geschehen wär bey dem kindlein. Er antwurt er west nichts das da geschehen oder geredt wär, wann wie er vor gesagt hat, da sprach der potestat zu im, er wär ein nar des er die warhait nit sagen wolt, vnd doch die andern gefangen Juden die gesagt hetten."
6. For Young Moses's interrogations, see YM, fols. 288–316. Here, see the interrogation of 9 November 1475, fols. 297, 303.
7. For the interrogations of Moses of Bamberg, see YM, fols. 354–88. Here, see fol. 369.
8. For Joaff's interrogations, see YM, fols. 220–49. Here, see fols. 220–24.
9. Interrogation of 27 October 1475, YM, fols. 226–27. The scribe of the YM copied the wrong date and wrote 17 instead of 27.
10. Interrogation of 27 October 1475, YM, fols. 225–26; two interrogations of 10 November 1475, fols. 236–37; interrogation of 11 November 1475, fols. 237–44; interrogation of 30 November 1475, fol. 246.

11. YM, fols. 339–41, 387.
12. YM, fols. 310–11.
13. YM, fols. 282–84.
14. YM, fol. 295.
15. YM, fols. 226, 264–67, 324.
16. YM, fols. 368, 370, 379.
17. YM, fol. 275.
18. YM, fol. 248.
19. YM, fols. 297–300.
20. YM, fols. 309, 333–34, 366.
21. YM, fols. 226, 247 (Joaff); fols. 260–67 (Isaac); fol. 297 (Young Moses); fols. 361, 364–65 (Moses of Bamberg).
22. YM, fols. 246, 267–72, 277–80, 296, 309, 331–32, 366–67.
23. YM, fols. 331–32.
24. YM, fols. 285–86, 313, 344–45, 376–80.
25. YM, fols. 378–79.
26. YM, fol. 285–86: Isaac was condemned as a "pluetfresser vnd trunker vnd Schmäher des allerheiligisten Leydens Jhesu Christi seiner göttlichen Mayestat vnd der allerhochgelobisten Junckfrawen Marie."
27. Carlo Ginzburg, *Storia notturna: Una decifrazione del sabba* (Turin, 1989), p. 279.
28. YM, fols. 379–80.
29. YM, fols. 380–85.
30. YM, fols. 228–233.
31. YM, fols. 311–13.
32. YM, fols. 336–38.
33. YM, fol. 270.
34. YM, fol. 272.
35. YM, fols. 278–80, 282.
36. YM, fol. 387.
37. YM, fol. 347: "Auff das sprach der potestat, seyt nun die vorgeschribne ding alle war wären, als er bekant vnd bestätt het, so solt er auff hebryschen geschrifft bey dem lebendigen waren got der himel vnd erden beschaffen hat, wie dann die Juden gewonhait haben sweren vnd doch nit anders, dann was war wär. Er antwurt, er wolt nit swern. Man fraget, warumb, er antwurt, es wär sünd vnd wie oft im der potestat fuursaget, so das war wär so solt er swern es wär nit sünd wann man die warhait swür, er antwurt er wolt nit swern es wär sünd."
38. YM, fol. 348.
39. YM, fols. 284–85.
40. YM, fols. 248–49, 315–16.
41. YM, fol. 390, interrogation of 12 April 1475.

CHAPTER NINE: THE CONVERT

1. YM, fol. 394.
2. YM, fol. 395.
3. YM, fol. 435.
4. YM, fol. 399: "Er sprach, O Jhesus, ich pin unschuldig, ich pitt den martrer als ich unschuldig pin, das er ein wunderzaichen thue."
5. YM, fols. 400–01.
6. YM, fols. 401–03.
7. YM, fol. 405.
8. YM, fols. 409–10.
9. YM, fols. 412–18. The scribe of the YM erroneously wrote "421" instead of "412."
10. YM, fols. 423–25.
11. For documents surrounding the 1476 Regensburg ritual murder trial, see Raphael Straus, ed., *Urkunden und Aktenstücke zur Geschichte der Juden in Regensburg, 1453–1738*. (Munich, 1960); for an analysis of the trial, see Hsia, *Myth of Ritual Murder*, pp. 72–82.
12. YM, fols. 427–34.
13. YM, fols. 428–31.
14. YM, fol. 432.
15. YM, fols. 434–45.
16. Israel's story is paraphrased rather than translated verbatim.
17. For Christian prejudices against Jewish converts, see Hans-Martin Kirn, *Das Bild vom Juden im Deutschland des frühen 16. Jahrhunderts* (Tübingen, 1989), pp. 62–66.
18. YM, fols. 445–46.
19. YM, fols. 447–49.
20. YM, fols. 449–52.
21. YM, fols. 452–55.
22. YM, fol. 456.
23. YM, fols. 456–61.
24. Gene Brucker, ed., *The Society of Renaissance Florence: A Documentary Study* (New York, 1971), doc. 119, 243–35.
25. On this bizarre episode see: AST, APV, SL, C. 69, no. 68.
26. YM, fols. 462–63.
27. YM, fols. 463–64.
28. YM, fols. 464–70.
29. YM, fols. 474–75: "Der tewfel het im geratten oder eyngebn solliche abgeschribne ding zethuen, darub er sich erkennet, das er den tod verschuld het, doch pät er das er im parmherzig wär vnd verurtaillet in zu einem schnellen tod damit er pald sturb."

30. The quotation is from the sentencing of Isaac, YM, fols. 285–86; for Lazarus's death sentence, see YM, fols. 348–49.
31. YM, fols. 249, 315–16, 476.
32. AST, APV, SL, C. 69, no. 63. This document appears in Ghetta, *Fra Bernardino*, 45–47.
33. YM, fol. 477.

CHAPTER TEN: THE WOMEN

1. W. P. Eckert, "Beatus Simonis: Aus den Akten des Trienter Judenprozesses," in W. P. Eckert and E. L. Ehrlich, eds., *Judenhass: Schuld der Christen? Versuch eines Gesprächs* (Essen, 1964), p. 345.
2. For Sara's interrogations, see YM, fols. 479–512. Here, fol. 481: "Sy hett von abgeng Irs hawswirts ir kranckhayt nit geliten. Ir sey auch der leyb groß gewesen. Doch wiß nit gewißleych ob sy schwanger sey oder nit."
3. YM, fol. 482.
4. On the religious subtext of medical views of menstruation in late medieval and early modern Europe, see Charles T. Wood, "The Doctors' Dilemma: Sin, Salvation, and the Menstrual Cycle in Medieval Thought," *Speculum* 56: 4 (1981), pp. 710–27; and Ottavia Niccolà, "'Menstruum Quasi Monstruum': Monstrous Births and Menstrual Taboo in the Sixteenth Century," in Edward Muir and Guido Ruggiero, eds., *Sex and Gender in Historical Perspective* (Baltimore, 1990), pp. 1–25.
5. For consultation on Sara's symptoms, I am indebted to Michael J. Langan, M.D. Letter from Michael J. Langan, M.D., to the author, 28 April 1991.
6. YM, fols. 483–84.
7. Testimony of Schönlein, 4 February 1476, YM, fols. 524–32. Here, fols. 530–31: "Sy war auch ir xviii jarn nye schwanger gewesen vnd hett nye kain frawen flus gehabt von der selbn zeyt her."
8. Possible medical explanations for Schönlein's medical history include Stein-Leventhal Syndrome (the thickening of the ovarian capsule thus preventing menstruation) and Turner's Syndrome (the congenital absence of ovaries). Letter from Michael J. Langan, M.D., to the author, 28 April 1991.
9. YM, fol. 506.
10. YM, fol. 533.
11. YM, fol. 568.
12. YM, fols. 479–81.
13. YM, fols. 483–85.
14. YM, fols. 488–93.
15. YM, fol. 494: "Antwurt man hett ir gestern versprochen, man wolt sy nymer fragn, man solt sy auch nymer fragn. Ir antwurt auch der Potestat, ob sy dye

warhayt nit sagn wolt, so wolt er ir lassen abziehn vnd pinden. Sy antwurt sy wolt nu dy warhayt sagn, so ir das an dem lebn nit schadn pracht. Der potestat sprach sy solt dy warhayt sagn vnd ließ sy auffziehn vnd pinden. Do antwurt sy ich sech das ir mein tod wellt vnd als man sy abzoch vnd pand da sprach sy, ir wellt etwas von mir wissen dar auß mir der tod get oder nachvolgt. Man sprach sy solt dy warhayt sagn, sy antwurt vnd fraget was dy bella oder dy schonlin bekannt het, der potestat sprach, sy het dy warhait verholn."

16. YM, fols. 494–97.
17. YM, fols. 513–17.
18. YM, fols. 520–24.
19. YM, fols. 497–98.
20. YM, fols. 534–38.
21. YM, fols. 507–08.
22. YM, fol. 546.
23. YM, fols. 603–11.
24. YM, fols. 569–73.
25. YM, fol. 528.
26. For descriptions of the women's role in food preparation, see YM, fols. 479, 485, 508a-b (Sara); fols. 517, 528 (Schönlein); fols. 558, 578 (Gütlein); fol. 591 (Anna).
27. YM, fols. 502–03, 538–39.
28. YM, fols. 542–43, 610–11.
29. YM, fols. 540–42.
30. YM, fol. 534.
31. YM, fol. 596.
32. YM, fol. 579: "Sy hatt auch die selbn wort da gesagt aber der potestat zu meyden grosser ubel wolt nit das man dy schrib." It was likely that there were Hebrew incantations against bad weather and ill health, but Gütlein's association of prophylactic magic with blood was meant to humor a judge eager to have his views of Jewish magic confirmed.
33. YM, fol. 562.

CHAPTER ELEVEN: JUDGMENT IN ROME

1. AST, APV, SL, C. 69, no. 70: "Venerabili Fratri, episcopo Tridentino. Sixtus P.M. Venerabilis Fratre Salutem et apud tuam bene. Post reditum venerabilis Fratris Baptiste episcopi Vintimiliensis quem ob causam hebreorum istuc misimus, cognitione huius cause quibusdam ex venerabilibus fratribus meis sanctae romanae ecclesiae cardinalibus commisimus, cuius commissionis vigore dudum inhibito emanavit, intelleximus tamen quod his non obstantibus, quottidie contra ipsos judeos aliquid innovas. In quo si ita sit, prudentiam

tuam miramur, qui non consideres id tibi, stante inhibitione huiusmodi non tuere, utcumque tamen sit, volumus, et sub pena suspensionis a divinis apostolica auctoritate tibi mandam ut deinceps huiusmodi occasione nihil contra judeos ipsos aut eorum aliquem debeas innovare, sed mulieres et vivos quos detines extra carceres in loco non incommodo, tuto tam servari facias, secus si fieret, quod non credimus materiam preberes tibi graviter succensendi. Datum Rome apud sanctum petrum sub annulo piscatoris die iii Aprilis M.CCCCLX-XVI pont. ma. anno quinto."

2. For the political history of Sixtus IV, see Ludwig von Pastor, *The History of the Popes,* vol. 4 (St. Louis, 1902); for cultural and intellectual history, see Charles L. Stinger, *The Renaissance in Rome* (Bloomington, 1985); Egmont Lee, *Sixtus IV and Men of Letters* (Rome, 1978); and the conference volume, *Un Pontificato ed una Città: Sisto IV (1471–1484),* ed. Massimo Miglio et al. (Vatican City, 1986).

3. Anna Esposito, "Gli Ebrei a Roma tra quattro e cinquecento," (Ebrei in Italia) *Quaderni Storici* 54 (December 1983), pp. 815–45; here, pp. 816–20.

4. Esposito, "Ebrei a Roma," pp. 822–23.

5. Kenneth R. Stow, *Taxation, Community and State: The Jews and the Fiscal Foundations of the Early Modern Papal State,* Päpste und Papsttum 19 (Stuttgart, 1982), p. 7.

6. Esposito, "Ebrei a Roma," p. 832; Stinger, *Renaissance in Rome,* pp. 53–54.

7. For Hinderbach's contacts to the Roman humanists, see the discussion below on Platina. After the publication of the papal bull in June 1478, Pomponius Laetus (Leto), the leader of the Roman Academy and a friend of Platina, wrote to congratulate Hinderbach as well. See AST, APV, SL, C. 69, no. 157. In addition, Hinderbach owned a copy of Biondo Falvio's "Italia illustrata," heavily notated in his own hand. See Jeffrey A. White, "Towards a Critical Edition of Biondo Flavio's 'Italia illustrata': a Survey and an Evaluation of the Manuscripts," in *Umanesimo a Roma nel Quattrocento* (Rome, 1984), p. 287.

8. King, *Venetian Humanism,* pp. 327–28; Pastor, *Popes,* 4: 121.

9. AST, APV, SL, C. 69, no. 62. Letter of Rottaler and Approvinus to Hinderbach, 12 January 1476.

10. AST, APV, SL, C. 69, no. 66.

11. AST, APV, SL, C. 69, no. 73.

12. AST, APV, SL, C. 69, nos. 71, 74, 77, 84, 97, 98.

13. AST, APV, SL. C. 69, nos. 76, 111.

14. AST, APV, SL, C. 69, no. 80a. This notarial instrument was drawn up by Johannes van den Dyck for the purpose of countering any claim that the women were forced into baptism. C. 69, no. 80b is a draft of 80a. The YM records that Gütlein was also baptized, as Justina, but there is no information on the date and circumstances of her baptism.

15. AST, APV, SL, C. 69, no. 82. Notarial instrument by Johannes van den Dyck (two copies).

16. AST, APV, SL, C. 69, no. 85.
17. Pastor, *Popes*, 4:411.
18. AST, APV, SL, C. 69, no. 110.
19. Stinger, *Renaissance in Rome*, pp. 8–9, 86, 189–90, 286; Pastor, *Popes*, 4: 433–35, 447–51.
20. Quaglioni, *Apologia Iudaeorum*, p. 110.
21. AST, APV, SL, C. 69, no. 122.
22. Quaglioni, *Apologia Iudaeorum*, p. 32.
23. Diego Quaglioni, "I Giuristi Medioevali e gli Ebrei. Due 'Consultationes' di G. F. Pavini (1478)," *Quaderni Storici* , N. S. 64 (April 1987), pp. 7–18. See also his *Apologia Iudaeorum*, pp. 32–35.
24. Quaglioni, *Apologia Iudaeorum*, p. 86: "Postremo dominaciones vestre diligenter actendant quale ex hoc negotio Tridentino periculum immineat religioni Christiane, et quales laquei rudibus et indoctis simplicibusque tendantur. Nam quemadmodum vera miracula ad fidei confirmationem a Deo sepe fieri compertum est, ita falsa et simulata et ingenio et arte humana conficta ad eius destructionem cedere sacri Ecclesie doctores non dubitant. Ideo antichristum non vera sed simulata miracula facturum ex sacris litteris commentatur: quia nulla sunt ad fidei destructionem validiora iacula, argumenta nulla forciora, nulli perniciosiores laquei ad decipiendum, quam huiusmodi falsorum miraculorum fictiones et fraudes. Vocant enim in dubium miracula apostolorum et martirum et veterum sanctorum, quos tamen constat veris et non fictis miraculis claruisse."
25. Quaglioni, *Apologia Iudaeorum*, p. 112: "Me sedente pro tribunali Roveredi, cum adesset Tridentinorum procurator non in angulo, sed palam in frequenti hominum conventu, ausus fuit protestari se ac Tridentinos illum suum beatum adorare tanquam secundum Christum, ut eius utar verbis, et tanquam secundum Messiam: quem preferebant, ut ille dicebat, omnibus virginibus, martiribus, apostolis et omnibus sanctis Ecclesie Dei. An tu posses ista, a quibus humane abhorrent aures, sine summa tua vituperatione defendere?"
26. André Vauchez, *La Sainteté en occident aux derniers siècles du moyen âge d'après le procès de canonisation et les documents hagiographiques* (Rome, 1981), pp. 176–77, 181–82.
27. The cardinals who served on the Commission, at one time or another, included Marco Barbo, Francesco Gonzaga, Giovanni Michiel, Giacomo Ammannati Piccolomini, Angelo Capranica, Ausia de Podio, Philibert Hugonet, and Francesco Todeschini Piccolomini. See Quaglioni, *Apologia Iudaeorum*, p. 35 n. 60 and Divina, *Storia*, 2: 178–79.
28. AST, APV, SL, C. 69, no. 83.
29. Pastor, *Popes*, 4: 408–14; Stinger, *Renaissance in Rome*, pp. 94–95.
30. AST, APV, SL, C. 69, no. 108.

31. AST, APV, SL, C. 69, no. 116. Letter of Rottaler to Hinderbach, 15 March 1478.

32. AST, APV, SL, C. 69, no. 119. Letter of Approvinus to Hinderbach, 24 March 1478. Approvinus learned of the rumor from Cardinal Barbo, who heard it from a Roman Jew, who heard it from the Jews in Rovereto.

33. AST, APV, SL. C. 69, no. 120.

34. AST, APV, SL, C. 69, no. 129; YM, fols. 1–3.

35. On the anti-Jewish polemic of the mendicant orders, see Jeremy Cohen, *The Friars and the Jews: The Evolution of Medieval Anti-Judaism* (Ithaca, 1982); on the relationship between Franciscan sermons against Jewish banking and the Monti di pietà, see the arguments of Renata Segre, "Bernardino da Feltre: I Monti di Pietà e i Banchi Ebraici," *Rivista Storica Italiana* 90 (1978), pp. 818–33. For a different view, see Anna Antoniazzi Villa, "A proposito di ebrei, francescani, Monti di Pietà: Bernardino de Bustis e la polemica antiebraica nella Milano di fine '400," in *Il Francescanesimo in Lombardia: Storia e Arte* (Milan, 1983), pp. 49–52.

36. See two articles by Dominique Rigaux: "L'immagine di Simone di Trento nell'arco alpino per il secolo XV: un tipo iconografico?" in Rogger, *Hinderbach*; and "Anitjudaïsme par l'image: L'iconographie de Simon de Trente (1475) dans la région de Brascia," in D. Tollet, ed., *Politique et religion dans le judaïsme ancien et médiéval* (Paris, 1990), pp. 309–17; see also Gabriella Ferri Piccaluga, "Economia, devozione e politica: immagini di Francescani amadeiti ed ebrei nel secolo XV," in *Francescanesimo in Lombardia*, pp. 107–22, esp. 109, ill. 28.

37. Cecil Roth, *The History of the Jews of Italy* (Philadelphia, 1946), pp. 172–73.

38. James S. Grubb, *Firstborn of Venice: Vicenza in the Early Renaissance State* (Baltimore, 1988), p. 97.

39. Laura dal Prà, "L'immagine di Simone di Trento nell'arte trentina dal secolo XV al secolo XVIII," in Rogger, *Hinderbach*.

40. Scherer, *Rechtsverhältnisse*, pp. 590–96.

41. Scherer, *Rechtsverhältnisse*, p. 614.

42. AST, APV, SL, C. 69, no. 137.

43. Bonelli, *Dissertazione*, p. 212a.

44. AST, APV, SL. C. 69, no. 1e.

45. Hermann Wiesflecker, *Kaiser Maximilian I: Das Reich, Österreich und Europa an der Wende zur Neuzeit*, vol. 4 (Munich, 1981), pp. 9–10.

46. Scherer, *Rechtsverhältnisse*, p. 615; Hsia, *Myth of Ritual Murder*, pp. 43–50; Kirn, *Das Bild vom Juden*, pp. 52–53.

47. Emanuela Trevisan-Semi, "Gli 'Haruge Trient' (Assassinati di Trento) e lo 'herem' di Trento nella tradizione ebraica," in Rogger, *Hinderbach*.

48. I rely on the English verse translation of the *Kinah* by Sylvia A. Herskowitz, in

Medieval Justice: The Trial of the Jews of Trent (New York, 1989). For the biblical references, I am indebted to Professor David Berger of Brooklyn College.

49. M[eir] Wiener, ed., *EMEK HABACHA von R. Joseph [ben Joshua] ha Cohen* (Leipzig, 1858), p. 63–64.
50. Quaglioni, *Apologia Iudaeorum*, p. 40.
51. *Processi*, pp. 86, 448–54.
52. *Processi*, p. 61, n. 22.

EPILOGUE

1. Esposito, "Lo stereotipo dell'omicidio," *Processi*, pp. 82ff.
2. Wagenseil's treatise, *Benachrichtigungen wegen einiger die Judenschafft angehenden wichtigen Sachen*, was published in Frankfurt-am-Main in 1705.
3. The original work, *Der Blutaberglaube in der Menschheit: Blutmorde und Blutritus* (Munich, 1892), was translated by Henry Blanchamp under the misleading title, *The Jew and Human Sacrifice* (New York, 1909).
4. For the encounter between Divina and Stern, see the preface of *Storia*. Moritz Stern's volume was published under the title: *Die päpstlichen Bullen gegen die Blutbeschuldigung* (Berlin, 1893).
5. *La Civiltà Cattolica*, XI, t.8 (1881), pp. 225–31, 344–52, 476–83, 598–606, 730–38; t.9 (1882), 107–113, 219–25, 353–62, 472–79, 605–13; t. 10 (1883), 727–38.
6. Menestrina, "Gli Ebrei a Trento," pp. 304–16, 384–411.
7. Volli, "I 'Processi Tridentini' e il Culto del Beato Simone da Trento."
8. W. P. Eckert, "Beatus Simoninus—aus den Akten des Trienter Juden-prozesses," in Eckert and Ehrlich, pp. 329–57.
9. In spite of this, the feast day of St. Simon is still listed in a Mexican church calendar, *164° Calendario del más Antiguo Galvan para el año de 1990*. I am indebted to John Harris (Weetangera, Australia) for this information.
10. The book by Elena Tessadri, *L'arpa di David: Storia di Simone e del Processo di Trento contro gli Ebrei accusati di omicidio rituale 1475–1476* (Milan, 1974), contains many errors and is not based on any of the extant manuscripts of the trial proceedings.

INDEX